THE
MALTESE
SPITFIRE

THE MALTESE SPITFIRE

ONE PILOT, ONE PLANE – FIND ENEMY FORCES ON LAND AND SEA

Sqdn. Ldr. HARRY COLDBECK D.F.C.

Airlife
England

Copyright © 1997 Harry Coldbeck

First published in the UK in 1997
by Airlife Publishing Ltd

British Library Cataloguing-in-Publication Data
A catalogue record for this book
is available from the British Library

ISBN 1 85310 878 2

Typeset by Hewer Text Composition Services, Edinburgh
Printed in England by St Edmundsbury Press Ltd,
Bury St Edmunds, Suffolk

Airlife Publishing Ltd
101 Longden Road, Shrewsbury, SY3 9EB, England.

CONTENTS

To Yvonne

ACKNOWLEDGEMENT

The author is grateful to all those who have helped him in the assembly and writing of this book. In particular, his wife Yvonne, Jim Berrett and Jack Bentinck-Stokes.

Jim Berrett, as has been mentioned, was himself a member of the early Malta Maryland crews and was instrumental in encouraging and assisting the author to set down his Spitfire experiences in that sphere.

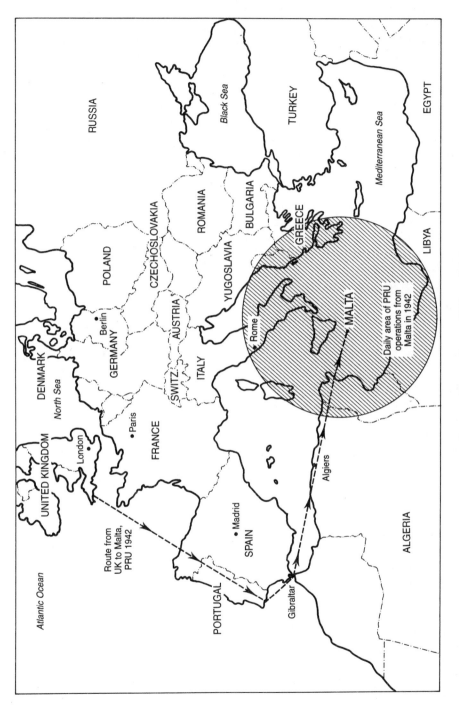

Route flown from UK to Malta

INTRODUCTION

'. . . *We get to know something about each other when we work together in this House. We see men with their qualities and defects . . .*'

Thus Winston Churchill on life in the House of Commons where he had spent most of his distinguished working life. Had he been a fighter pilot (and one could imagine the role attracting him), he could well have said the same thing about serving in a combat unit in wartime. For there we did indeed see people as they really were – not as some extrovert caricature of themselves.

In the rough autumn and winter days of 1941, in No 66 Squadron of Fighter Command of the Royal Air Force (a nasty time in the air war on the Western Front), we got to know the author of this book for what he genuinely was – an utterly dependable, constant and determined New Zealander with whom just a twinkle of humour was never far away. Everyone liked Harry Coldbeck in 66 Squadron.

But he was not a fighter pilot in the image that the rest of us were. It wasn't his scene. He was, in truth, never intended to be there. He found himself unexpectedly in a famous old fighter squadron by one of those earlier quirks of posting which went curiously wrong. When he set out from his native land to fight for King and Country, his large-sized heart was bent upon becoming a bomber pilot, a role for which his finely tuned judgement and calculating mind would have been exceptionally well suited.

Quietly undemonstrative and without those mercurial, sparkling and – yes – somewhat unstable qualities which we came to associate with the day-fighting art, Harry was never going to be by nature, as the cliché has it, 'one of us.' But what he did do by his honesty, character, personality and resolve was to take his place in the line and acquit himself as a respected and valued member of the unit. He applied himself doggedly – and devotedly – to the task of fitting himself for a part for which the Good Lord had surely not intended him.

And strange things . . . way-out things . . . always seemed to happen to him as if to call attention to the fact that he wasn't really cast in that mould. Who else, for instance, would ever have had the unnerving experience of the throttle handle of his Spitfire actually coming off – *right off* – in his hand in the middle of an operation? (He tells the story quite splendidly among the pages which follow.) It could have been disastrous, fatal; yet such was Harry Coldbeck's skill as a pilot, and his iron control over his temperament, that, somehow, he contrived to land his aircraft safely.

'It couldn't have happened,' as the saying goes, 'to a nicer man.' And when he came to recount, with his usual objective honesty, this appalling experience the other members of his Flight could barely contain their laughter . . . *Because it had happened to Harry. And to no one else!*

Then one day, the author of this arresting story got the break for which his undoubted genius intended him. A signal came through from Command and Group inviting one of the Squadron's pilots to volunteer for photographic reconnaissance duties (PRU) – an exacting, taxing, testing job of endurance if ever there was one.

The author didn't hesitate. His judgement and sense of purpose – and what attributes they proved later to be – were quickly at work. They told him instantly that this was the slot for him. But when he took two paces forward and offered to fill the void, the whole Squadron was cast down; we didn't want him to go despite knowing that this was probably right for him. Such was the affection in which he was held. The man had endeared himself to us . . .

The rest is history told in the story which follows with an attractive modesty which lays bare the trials that studded the forward path.

Those of us who saw his work close to in the tenuous Mediterranean days of 1942, when the pressures were being loaded upon him, will never forget the professional competence he displayed in obtaining the intelligence for which his blue Spitfire's cameras had been expressly designed.

The truth is that his achievements (and those of his indomitable comrades, Les Colquhoun[1] and Jo Dalley[2] whose commission he secured) far exceeded in importance the level he accords them in this account. In this, his style is in plain contrast with the flamboyance of his highly-publicised contemporary, Adrian Warburton – 'Warby'

1 Sergeant, later Squadron Leader L.R. Colquhoun DFC, GM, DFM,
2 Flight Sergeant, later Group Captain J.O. Dalley OBE, DFM, RAF, (Ret'd)

– for whom Malta, as a rare theatre, might have been specially prepared.

None was better placed than Coldbeck to observe at first hand Warburton's idiosyncratic traits. His revealing assessment, sharply at variance with the widely accepted impression created by the legend, is thus of capital significance for the historical record.

An altogether new picture of this lone, unpredictable, aloof and sometimes strangely uncaring character starts to emerge. Questions, hitherto unthought of, will now begin to be asked. To the mystery of Warburton's loss later in the war on a photographic reconnaissance mission to southern Germany from the UK will inevitably be added fresh queries concerning some aspects of his glamorous operational career.

Such is the reliability of Harry Coldbeck's witness that a few, looking closely, may even dare to think the unthinkable. Limited though it is, the New Zealander's evidence points to an unexpected slant upon the war-time memory of one of the Royal Air Force's – and Malta's – favourite sons.

It will certainly raise a few eyebrows and generate some heat. This is all to the good. There is nothing like a dash of argument and controversy to challenge the record . . .

Wing Commander P. B. 'Laddie' Lucas, CBE, DSO, DFC
London, March 1995

CHAPTER ONE

EARLY DAYS

As a very small boy in the early 1920s, I watched aeroplanes
flying over my home in Christchurch, New Zealand, leaving
a trail of dark smoke. On later flights the smoke was no
longer to be seen but the changes intrigued me, a young lad, who
knew nothing of aviation but who was keenly interested. It was to be
many years before I would be close to aircraft with the heady aroma
of aircraft fabric dope, glue and aviation fuel but my interest in all
flying and aeroplanes had been born and it was to lead to many
years of enjoyable experience.

I later learned that the aircraft I saw, as a young boy, were probably
the Avro 504K from Sockburn, on the perimeter of Christchurch, the
airfield which eventually became known as 'Wigram'. The change
from smoke trails to no smoke trails was, in one case, probably due
to the change of aircraft from the ancient radial-powered Avro 504Ks
to the Rolls-Royce in line Falcon of the Bristol fighters of greatly
differing design.

I was about five or six when I began to make elementary models in
straw, of the flying machines I could see overhead. These models with
round fuselages were made from flax stalks, which were easily shaped
and the wings and tails from stout straw; non-flying of course.

When I was about eleven or twelve and now living in Merivale,
Christchurch, I joined a Model Club with the pretentious name of
'The Society of Model Aircraft Engineers'. The Society met formally
under the presidency of a Mr Gunther, a hairdresser in Colombo
Street. The models of the time were mainly rubber-powered and only
suitable for flying in light winds or calm conditions. The President
usually led from the front, with his regularly performing creation,
the 'Kinglet'. This English designed model, with a single surface low
wing, was beautifully crafted from mainly spruce which was covered
in oiled silk.

Mr Gunther had ingeniously devised a parachute device for the
'Kinglet'. Before the launching, a parachute would be folded and

put in a pack beneath the fuselage. At the moment of launch Mr Gunther would, with the end of his cigarette, ignite a fuse which was timed to release the weighted parachute at a suitable height and which drifted down to the junior spectators' delight. He also had made a splendid petrol motor powered model which was mainly on display in his shop. I did not see this one in flight.

With my particular friend, Noel Baty, a boy of about my own age, I made many models with varying degrees of success in flying them. In my case, I was working under difficulty as I had no workshop and very little pocket-money to buy materials. We obtained plans from various sources – mainly English and American modelling magazines which we borrowed and passed around after the chosen plans were traced. (Photo-copying had yet to be invented). We also made scale models and these flew too. Whilst I favoured the DH 60 Moth, Noel was more inclined to the SE5A. There were other models, some of our own design, which we flew. More usually, the wrecks were taken home for repair at the end of the 'flying' time. The prevailing North Easterly winds, sea breeze, were a nuisance so it was often necessary to fly in the early morning when calmer conditions prevailed.

Noel and I had first become acquainted when another friend, of my school days, John Prosser, invited me to a field meeting of the Canterbury Glider Club, near Christchurch, where he was keen to show me Noel's ingeniously repaired bicycle. In the main, in those days, our means of surface transport was on our 'bikes'. It appears Noel had crashed his bike during a tour on the West Coast and in order to continue, he had employed pieces of timber in conjunction with No. 8 fencing wire, to good effect and here he was still using it in this emergency mode, some time later.

The Glider Club was operating from a field on the Van Ash estate, at the lower Cashmere Hills and the headquarters were at the back of the President's contracting premises, which was on the same property as the President, Mr Bell's, residence. This was where the Zögling Primary Glider had been built and it was returned at the end of flying and for repair which, more often than not, was the same thing. The Zögling was a most elementary aircraft where the pilot, restrained by a seat belt around his waist, sat out in the front with his hand on the stick and his feet on the rudder bar. There were no instruments except a moving spring-loaded plate facing forward which showed air speed against a calibrated plate on the underside of the wing. The monoplane wing atop the frame fuselage was braced to a cabane with flying and landing wires extending out to the top and bottom of about mid wing. These wires sang in flight, in this type of aircraft, according to air speed and gave the pilot audible indication of air speed – (or lack of it).

My interest in flying was bolstered by the proximity of a means to fly and although, for financial reasons, I did not belong to the club, my presence was always welcome as a helper with the catapult and helping to retrieve the glider by pulling it up the hill after it had landed in the valley below.

The catapult consisted of bungee cords in the form of a large Vee with a ring at the joining point. The other two ends were finished with rope handholds. There was room for four or five persons pulling the end of each of these ropes. The drill usually was to locate the glider for take-off on high ground facing a suitable take-off area into wind. The tail was fastened to a lever-controlled hook and one person was detailed to operate the release on a hand or verbal signal from the pilot. The team on each end of the launching bungee would walk out, away from the glider, then as they took up the strain, they would trot, then run. The pilot, at a suitable moment of bungee tension, would signal to the person stationed at his rear to release and away the glider would go with bracing wires singing, on a gentle glide to the valley below and, hopefully, a good landing.

These halcyon picnic-like flying days were cut short when some miscreants vandalised a farm tool shed on the estate and the Glider Club was understandably asked to find another flying area. Fortunately the Club was granted permission to use Wigram airfield on Sundays when no powered flying was taking place. The use of the bungee launch was very limited on the flat so a towed launch became the norm. Mr Bell, the Club President, was the owner of a circa 1924 Studebaker Tourer which he generously allowed to become the towing vehicle. The glider joined by a long tow rope to the car was towed until sufficient height was gained and the pilot then released the tow rope which fell away and the landing could be made into wind inside the airfield boundary. Mr Bell would then tow the glider back downwind for another launch. This was basic flying.

One Sunday, the pilot whose turn it was to fly the glider was reputed to have been a pilot in the Royal Flying Corps in World War 1. He was, however, difficult to talk to about aeronautical matters and he would not go into detail about his previous flying experiences. On this Sunday, during his flight at Wigram, he appeared to get out of wind and on his approach to landing, moved into a side slipping stalled condition and crashed. The glider was in a terrible mess and I do not think I ever saw it flying again. The pilot wandered off and he had to be searched for – being eventually found in a dazed state and taken to his home.

The basic frame of the fuselage and wings was wood, usually spruce, which in the case of the wings and tail surfaces was covered in balloon fabric, doped to give it the required tension. The fuselage frame was uncovered. It was in the process of many repair sessions at Mr Bell's premises that amateurs of the time like John, Noel and myself discovered and used casein glue and the process of applying wrinkle-free fabric and the stabbing process. The 'stabbing' referred to was usually carried out by two members or helpers positioned either side of the fabric-covered wing which was standing on its leading or trailing edge. One of these operators would pass a very long threaded needle through the fabric, alongside a wing rib, to the opposite person who would reverse and stab the needle back again on the other side of the rib. The first operator would then make a join in the loop which was now through the fabric around the rib. This loop, after being repeated many times on the many ribs of the wing, ensured that the fabric remained remained in contact, thereby complying with the aerofoil shape of the wing in flight.

From time to time, John Prosser and I, or Noel Baty and I, visited Wigram to watch any flying taking place, usually at weekends when we could get away, there being only club flying. There were, however, always the Air Force hangars where we could look through the windows at the types on the establishment of what was, in those days, called the 'New Zealand Permanent Air Force'. The Gloster Grebes were the most fascinating biplane single-seat fighter we had ever seen and we were always especially keen to cycle the ten miles or so out there if one of them was likely to be outside the hangar. Following closely, in our young estimation, was the Bristol Fighter F2B which while of a 1917 design, had covered itself with glory and had a great reputation in World War 1. It was still in service.

Other more modern designs which also have since long gone, were Hawker Tom Tits, Avro 626s and a frequent visitor, domiciled at Auckland, the Fairey lllF. There was also a family of de Havilland types such as the DH 60 Moth, Puss Moth and DH 50. All these interesting aircraft types and pieces of equipment made the time between cycling the ten miles out and back again go so very quickly.

On Air Force field days or when special events were taking place, there was often an opportunity to see the 'Hucks Starter' in action. This was a device mounted on a Model T Ford chassis for engaging a coupling at the airscrew boss and turning the airscrew to start the Rolls-Royce Falcon engine and the Jaguar engine of the Grebe.

There was no security to speak of nor was any needed and it is interesting to remember that in those days some time before World War II, members of the Air Force in New Zealand went to work in their own civilian clothes and lived away from the station in their own houses or apartments. Uniform, when supplied was generally worn on special occasions like 'Open Days' and when VIPs were visiting.

There were flying accidents from time to time and two which I remember being reported involved a Bristol Fighter and another a Gloster Grebe. In the case of the Bristol, the pilot of the Territorial Air Force was flying without his corrected goggles when he flew into the ground target at Lake Ellesmere.

The Gloster Grebe fighter had been converted to a two-seater, which it was said, failed in flight to recover from a flat spin. The pilot, Squadron Leader Finley and passenger, Aircraftman Simpson, were badly injured and Simpson sadly lost his sight. It was understood at the time that a similarly converted to two-seater Grebe, resulted in a crash in comparable circumstances in the UK. Later information, however, suggests that a dual Grebe was allocated to each RAF Grebe Squadron. There was a single-seater in RNZAF service until 1938. As the possibility of war approached in 1936 the Director of Air Services in New Zealand was Squadron Leader T.M. Wilkes, who advocated that the Labour Government of the time obtain the services of an expert from the Royal Air Force to reform the Air arm of the armed services in New Zealand.

Wing Commander the Hon. R.A. Cochrane AFC, RAF, was appointed to organise the RNZAF and he, as Group Captain, was soon appointed it first Chief of Staff, 1937–1939.

As a Wing Commander, he had been on his organising term for only a short time when he was able to make up his mind quickly about what was required to bring the existing air arm, of about 100 personnel, to what would be a realistic force of men and machines.

Whose idea it was I do not know, whether it was Cochrane's or the Government's but about this time the Wing Commander addressed anyone interested in the revisions to the Air Force at an evening meeting in the Chamber of Commerce, Christchurch. I was delighted – admission was free and it was an 'out of this world' experience to hear the projected plans directly from the author of them, delivered in a most straightforward, lucid and matter of fact way. I was about 19 on this memorable occasion.

Some long time afterwards for me an exciting aspect of preparations for the threatened war was the formation of a Civil Air Reserve similar to that being formed in the United Kingdom. Applicants, when accepted, were to be given some 40 hours' training during the first year, with refresher courses of 10 hours or so each subsequent year. This was at no cost to the trainee nor it seems, was there any obligation to join the Air Force, as was shown when I later met two who had, instead, joined the Army on the outbreak of war. My application to join was rejected. No reason was given.

The first time I had personally taken to the air was in 1933 in a DH 60M. The 'M' indicated it was a metal Moth. These metal Moths had a metal fuselage frame with stringers which were covered in fabric giving it a more rounded appearance than the rather squarish DH 60G which was a wooden Moth.

The flight being referred to here was a very exciting event for me and had been arranged by a Miss Ashbey through her friends, the Broughtons. Their son, Flying Officer Charlie Broughton, a Cranwell College RAF cadet, was home on leave from his RAF Wapiti Squadron based at Risalpur in India – (the area now known as Pakistan).

We met as pre-arranged and motored out to Wigram in his little Triumph 8hp which tended to buzz along with its high revving engine. At Wigram, the aircraft we were to use, a silver DH 60M was ready and the two of us climbed aboard. He, the pilot, was in the back cockpit with me in the front one. The flight was all I could have wished for, combining, as it did, great views of the countryside, the mountains and the sea and sky. Finally, Charlie did some aerobatics and a couple of spins. After landing I offered to reimburse him for the hire of the aircraft but he waved that off. Much later I found out that it was Miss Ashbey who was my benefactor. As well as arranging the flight she had paid for it. She was a wonderful friend to me in my youthful years and I remember her with great gratitude. Incidentally, the pilot on this my memorable first flight, on the last occasion when I saw him, was a Group Captain. Subsequent information reveals that he is now Air Marshal Sir Charles Broughton, KBE, CB, RAF (Retired).

One of the most important events which affected my life both physically and mentally had occurred about this time. Enjoying my emancipation from parental interdicts, at the age of seventeen years, entirely self-supporting but only just managing financially, I went along with John Prosser to join the Union Rowing Club situated on the Avon River in Christchurch. We were introduced to the club skiffs and given rowing instruction and trial runs, all of which was absorbing and interesting but to my disappointment it was revealed I had a congenital double hernia.

Once again John took the lead and on our bikes we set off for Opawa, a suburb of Christchurch and the rooms where John knew of a Dr Taylor. After examination and discussing the pros and cons, Dr Taylor gave me his pragmatic advice and a note to take to the hospital on the other side of town. His advice was that I should have an operation without delay. On our bikes again. Arriving, we stayed in the waiting area, fairly quiet at that time of day (early evening), and I was called in for an examination by a house surgeon this time who asked me if I could come, (be admitted) straight away. Whereupon John offered to take my ramshackle bicycle home to the Hall family where I was boarding and that evening I went to bed in Ward 4, Christchurch Hospital.

This, being in a strange bed in a long ward with about a dozen beds arranged along both walls with tables down the middle, was an entirely new experience, as was the fact that one of the occupants died during the night. Next day, the Hall family, alerted by John, brought me my small kit and other convenience essentials. I also made the acquaintance of the nurse in charge of the Ward – a Sister Manson.

Next day there seemed to be all sorts of physical examinations, meals in bed and other fascinating procedures such as the barber. Eventually, after a journey, being wheeled prostrate on a trolley, I was lying on the operating table looking up at the special lamps and the ceiling. To my surprise, Sister Manson's face appeared close to mine and she said, 'I can't find anyone who will take responsibility for your operation, will you?' I said, 'Of course I would', thinking she meant the physical aspect. I was to discover it was the bill to which she was referring and I was presented with that as I left, bent over, after about a fortnight. The amount was something over about fifty pounds which I paid off slowly for some time to come until the Hospital Board wrote off the last part. In those days some people belonged to Lodges and other friendly societies which insured them against such unexpected medical expenses.

My employer of the time, Mr C.A. Cooper of Victoria Street, kindly paid my wages during my time in hospital and for the two weeks' convalescence which the doctor advised on my discharge from the hospital.

John Prosser's mother and father arranged for me to stay with John's aunt in Timaru and while there I quickly regained my normal good health.

Unfortunately, the beneficent Mr Claude Cooper died while I was overseas on World War II service.

As a preliminary to undertaking flying instruction, in New Zealand in the thirties, one had to pass the appropriate medical examination.

This was taken privately and the doctor filled in the form provided and then sent it off to the Air Department in Wellington. In my case, I went to Dr Scott in Christchurch who was in fact the police doctor and, therefore, used to such service-type formalities. Dr Scott was a well-known figure to me, driving his circa 1932 Dodge saloon, with the inevitable cigarette in place in his mouth. His consulting rooms too had the aroma of tobacco smoke. As Dr Scott put me through the various tests and examinations he proffered a medical bottle and said, 'Pump ship into that'. It was the first time I had heard that expression. I then proceeded to identify a series of coloured woollen 'Board of Trade Tufts' which he said he used for colour vision testing mariners for their various tickets. Later, Air Force colour vision testing was done with the Ishihara book of dotted figures and its ability to demonstrate deficiencies in an examinee's colour recognition. Nevertheless, I have known keen-type aspiring flyers who have learned the pages off by heart so that it appears the system could be manipulated – if the aspirant worked on it hard enough.

My medical examination concluded, I then had to wait for the result to come through from the Air Department before I could start even dual instruction in the air. The doctor had said he had passed me fit and to my own satisfaction I realised that Dr Taylor, the hospital, the expense and all the aggravation of my surgery had brought my physical requirements satisfactorily into line, albeit at the end of my 'teen years. I was not to know that that was not the last I would know of that type of surgery.

I had, meanwhile, been keeping myself abreast of aviation matters as far as possible and I now decided that I would join the Canterbury Aero Club and learn to fly to licence standard. The fees for flying tuition seem small by today's standards; at £3 per hour for dual on DH 60 Moths up to the first 3 hours solo, then £2 per hour solo – tradesmen's wages at the time were about 2/6 an hour or £5 for the 40-hour week, which had just been established countrywide by the Savage Government.

The Aero Club's main training machines were DH 60 G&M plus a two-seat Miles Hawk which was equipped with full instrument flight panels, front and back cockpit with a hood on the rear cockpit. The Hawk was more expensive, by the hour. Another Miles aircraft in the fleet was the three-passenger cabin Whitney Straight which was popular with passengers and pilots alike and was very busy on field days. These field days were held from time to time and were advertised in the *Press*, the main Christchurch newspaper. As well as the advertisements, club pilots flew in formation over Christchurch to remind potential patrons of the availability of passenger flights in club aircraft. On special occasions flying displays were also programmed. On the field days, senior club pilots as well as the staff flying instructors would be busy carrying out passenger flights in these aircraft and boosting their hours on type, augmented at one time by a Fox Moth and subsequently the Monospar. The twin-engined Monospar seated four including, I think from memory, the pilot.

Junior club pilots like myself were usually busy escorting passengers out to the aircraft and ensuring they were safely seated and securely fastened in by the safety belt. We also showed them how to get out in a hurry if necessary.

My flying instructors at this time were an interesting study. One instructor affected a long cigarette holder and offered little in the way of tuition. 'OK taxy out, take off and climb up. Turn here, turn again to the left and land. Taxy back and take off again'. The free-lance aviator who was the second instructor, niggled from the moment of starting. Extracts from a twenty minute schooling period sounded like 'Don't taxy so fast; you'll have to taxy faster or we'll never get airborne. Don't open the throttle so far; Open the throttle wider. Now turn right, that's too far'. Phew!

The third tutor was a retired motorcyclist of some renown who from the pupil's point of view had the most rapport and I tried to juggle my flying bookings to coincide with his duty times. Len Poore, who after I had had a total of five hours dual flying instruction and on a calm evening when I had cycled out to Wigram as fast as my bicycle would go, after the third landing, told me to stop. I had carried out three circuits and landings on this calm summer evening with smoke from an adjacent chimney going straight up. As the Moth came to a halt, the little door on the front cockpit sprang open and the bulk of the instructor started to climb out. Then, having removed the front stick and secured the seat belt and his door, he came down to my cockpit and put the stick in the locker just to the rear of me. He said, 'OK, go off and do one on your own, as you have been doing'. So off I went and did another circuit with a strange but reassuring feeling that somehow the instructor, Len, was still in the front cockpit. I made a good landing and when I had taxied back to the parking area I climbed out and felt as though I was walking on air and my feet not touching the ground. I'd gone solo!

Back in the flight office signing in for my solo and settling up for the dual and solo time, my instructor was saying, 'It's just a first solo' – apparently to dispel any incipient over-confidence.

Checking in at the desk was another first soloist, but this one, who always seemed considerably older, even elderly, had been taking an enormous number of dual hours before finally making it. He, like me, was very pleased. I understood he was a lawyer in the City and obviously, unlike me, funding his long tuition was not a problem. He climbed into his smart saloon car while I cycled off on my bike. Next morning, sadly, his death notice was in the morning paper. Presumably due to natural causes.

My flying routine from now, consisted of a check flight and solo, until I had totalled three hours on my own. All this was on the DH 60G. We had two very new DH 60Gs which was really becoming an obsolete type, being out of production. These two Moths, ZK-AGU and ZK-AGV had been built by the apprentices at the de Havilland base at Hatfield, in southern England and had been purchased for the Canterbury Aero Club by the secretary, Mr Climie, while on tour in England. The DH 82 Tiger Moth had virtually replaced the DH 60 Gipsy Moth as a trainer but at Canterbury we had the DH 60s of various ages, some like ZK-AAR and ZK-AAW were quite old but we also had these two new Gipsies. There were no Tigers on the Club establishment at pre-war Wigram.

In my experience, the DH 60G was very light and required more skill to land perfectly than the Tiger. Unlike the 60M or Tiger, the 60G had a fixed tail skid and turning into wind with the downwind boundary looming up, required positive bursts of throttle to lift the tail around. This was sometimes daunting to the inexperienced novice.

A total of three hours solo was required before a student pilot could leave the vicinity of the airfield. During this period he had to remain within a three mile radius. After that he was required to maintain an altitude of two thousand feet over the City and countryside, (e.g. friends' houses and other places of interest).

Airfield control in those days was largely non-existent, in that a pilot was required to obey the International Rules of the Air, superimposed on good airmanship. A pilot controlled his own, and to some extent, others' destinies, by being constantly aware of what was going on all around, on the ground and in the air – it was called airmanship which was contributed to by one's own experience, by reading and by learning from other pilots of greater experience.

During the time I was buying flying instruction as a member of the Canterbury Aero Club, I shared instructors and facilities with members of the now established Civil Air Reserve. However, their instruction, which cost them nothing, was much more sophisticated and they enjoyed experience on the more expensive machines such

21

as the Miles Hawk for instrument flight practice which was also provided.

There were lectures on flying subjects laid on at the club rooms in the evenings from time to time and I think they were mainly for Civil Air reservists but I used to attend by cycling out to Wigram, or ride on the tram, if the snow or the weather was too tough, especially in the winter. The lecturers took as their subjects, Air Regulations, Navigation, Aircraft Maintenance, Inspection, Signals, Meteorology and General Airmanship. Eventually I had put in enough air time to be able to take the 'A' licence test of flying and oral examinations.

I knew what the test consisted of because, at the time, it was the same as the UK syllabus, details of which I already had in my possession.

On the appointed week-day, I presented myself at the Canterbury Aero Club flight office and the pleasant receptionist/cashier and general factotum directed me to the Duty Pilots' Hut over on the Air Force Area and Flying Officer Dive, who could be seen standing outside.

Flying Officer Dive and I exchanged pleasantries and then he proceeded to examine my knowledge of Air Regulations, a little meteorology and general airmanship. He afterwards directed me to return to the club for my test aircraft which I had booked and I informed him which one it would be with the large distinguishing registration letters which he could see from the distance. He had briefed me about the three figures-of-eight I would have to perform across the airfield at 500 feet and then land on the circle using the engine.

The second part of the test was to take off again and climb to two thousand feet, over the airfield, close the throttle and glide down, landing on the circle again not using power except to clear the spark plugs occasionally.

After landing the second time I taxied back to the parking area then walked over to Flying Officer Dive who was waiting for me and he rewarded me with the news that I had passed my 'A' licence test. As on the first solo, I was highly elated. My 'A' licence entitled me to fly anywhere in an aircraft annotated on my licence but not to carry passengers or fly for hire or reward. The 'anywhere' was of course conditioned by the Club instructional staff authorising a pilot to hire the aircraft, so it was quite regulated really.

As stated from time to time the aero club held field days at which the general public were invited and who could buy trips in the club aircraft. All the serviceable DH 60 Moths and, at one time, the Fox Moth, the Miles Whitney Straight, the Miles Hawk and the Monospar were available. There was also the Piper Cub on loan from Barney Owen, a prominent club member and city chemist known as Cook and Ross's.

Suitably qualified senior club pilots were only too pleased to increase their flying hours free, helping the staff instructors by flying passengers for 'joy rides'. Junior pilots, like me, spent all the day escorting passengers in and out and fastening them into the aircraft and extracting them again on landing. My first long distance flight, in fact the first time I had been out of the South Island, was as a passenger in the club Monospar.

Union Airways, the internal passenger airline in NZ at that time, was establishing a large base at Milson, Palmerston North, and at the date of the formal opening of this facility, the Canterbury Aero Club, along with other contemporary clubs, planned to be represented on the big day. It was arranged that our club would send the Monospar. The Chief Instructor was the pilot and I was invited to be one of three fare-paying passengers.

It was for me, a most interesting flight from Wigram to Palmerston North. After arrival we were given a most informative tour of the workshops by the chief engineer and then there was the formal opening ceremony of what seemed to me to be a very grand building. The DH 86, four-engined Express Airliners were the aircraft in use. Afterwards there was a certain amount of celebration and finally the night at the hotel in town into which we had previously booked.

Next morning there was a bustling about on the airfield as everybody prepared themselves and their aircraft for homeward flights. An Oxford aircraft and crew, representing the Air Force, were ready to go early and they took off. The Oxford, at that time, was a new aircraft and of great interest to those who had not been near one previously. The pilot officer flying it, apparently decided to do a low fly past. As it came in low there was a loud 'thwack,' after which the Waco cabin biplane which had been warming up on my left was switched off. It appears, after take-off and climbing up, the Oxford wireless operator had lowered the trailing aerial and that trailing lead-weighted wire had seriously damaged the Waco whose crew must have had to find other means of getting home that day.

CHAPTER TWO

AIR FORCE TRAINING

D aily at this time, early 1939, the War, or possibility of it, occupied much space in the newspapers and in our conversations. The Munich Crisis had passed but in spite of Mr Chamberlain's 'peace in our time', the threat of war was still very real.

I had applied to join the Civil Air Reserve but lacking any influence or great sporting or other achievement, I was not accepted for all that lovely flying tuition which those who were accepted, enjoyed. Enjoyed may be the wrong description because I met a couple of them during the war and they had joined the Army for their war service, not the Air Force.

September 1939 and war had come to pass and recruiting for aircrew was taking place. This time when I applied I was notified to report to King Edward Barracks in Cashel Street, Christchurch, for an interview by a selection board.

The president of the selection panel, I remember, was sitting in sunlight, at the table with his flying badge and ribbons looking most colourful on his blue uniform. At the left-hand end of the table sat a smiling civilian, in morning suit, who invited me to take a seat. Questions followed, mainly from the Air Force officer president, but also from the civilian who I believe was Mr Caradus, Director of Education. The president asked if I had flown to which I replied, 'Yes'. Next question, 'How much?' Reply, I have my 'A' licence. After an expression of surprise I was handed a card with Airman Pilot U/T* on it which was all I desired at that moment.

With the arrival of the month of May, another step was taken in the direction of flight – attestation into the armed services.

Meanwhile, the powers that be had decided that since we had volunteered for active service when the war started, it seemed hardly fair that in mid-1940, we were still in civilian clothes. It was decided,

* Under training.

therefore, to issue each of us with a numbered 'V' badge to show that we were volunteers who were attested and waiting for our flying course to start. The 'V' badge was a Roman capital letter with a fern entwined and there were many signatures and other measures taken to ensure it was returned as soon as we were in uniform and not given away as a souvenir.

From about May 1940, those of us now selected had to attend a course at the Christchurch Technical School, designed by Mr Caradus, and we covered such subjects as mechanics and physics, mathematics, meteorology and navigation. This was a very high quality course and I was glad that, pre-war, I had attended a tutor's rooms in Victoria Street, where I had undertaken a refresher course of study to bring me up to School Certificate standard. This enabled me to cope well with the Air Force course and final examinations.

Eventually, in December 1940, my posting to the Ground Training School at Levin came through and I took my travel voucher for train and inter-island steamer to Levin to join number 10 aircrew course. Pay was to be at the special rate of £150 per annum.

At Levin there was all the usual documentation, medical exams and the issue of uniforms, with boots and shoes as well as shirts. The vaccination and other injections were attended to also. Drill started and it wasn't long before dressing drill, with the necessity to touch the shoulder of one's neighbour, found the maturing vaccination area very painful.

Drill, Physical Training (PT) and Ground studies, were taken alternately; one day, morning drill with afternoon studies, next day, morning studies, afternoon drill/PT. In 1940, I remember, during the very hot weather of our summer, the Medical Officer had us shifted off the tarmac parade ground to the large grass playing fields to practise drill as well as PT.

Discipline for us was very strict and the uniform we wore as aircrew under training was distinguished by a white flash in the front of the forage cap. Any slight misdemeanour around the camp or elsewhere was rewarded with extra duties such as cleaning out ditches and other fatigues.

Our quarters were tents, in immaculate lines. The tents had plain board floors, raised off the ground with board sides half way up the walls. Two to a tent with a clothes hanging space at the end of each bed. The housekeeping of the occupants had to be perfect and the tent left with sides rolled up ready for inspection each morning.

Some of the regular camp staff were found guilty of misbehaviour in the local town of Levin and one who had apparently been involved in window smashing was awarded 'pack drill' as corporal punishment. This punishment was somewhat barbaric by today's standards and the offender had to don all his equipment, complete with water bottle and rifle, in the hot sun. Several drill corporals were required to drill him while we were lined up and made to watch as a salutary lesson although we had had nothing to do with the original offence.

Social life at that time was almost non-existent but I do remember a very pleasant visit to the coastal beach, by service transport, one weekend. A big feature of that day was gathering of toheroas which were new to me and collecting was un-restricted in those days. The cooks, or chefs, as they have now become known, made a wonderful soup which was enjoyed by all on the station. The toheroa is a succulent shellfish.

One weekend, on leave, we were walking down the Levin main street and took advantage of a large notice outside a tailoring establishment. The notice against which we lined up for a photograph, read 'Girls Wanted'. We weren't very successful.

At the end of the course on 8 February 1941, we were keen to know to which Elementary Flying Training School we would be posted for the *ab initio* flying training. There was a short leave interval and then I reported to Harewood on the outskirts of Christchurch. I found Harewood greatly changed from the Aero Club days at Wigram and the now dilapidated club rooms looked forlorn in their new setting.

A large new hangar had been built there with new accommodation blocks. A new messing complex, with what is known in other climes, as the NAAFI, in the form of the YMCA with its reading and writing rooms and recreational facilities. It was now a very smart station equipped with a Watch Tower and all the safety services. No. 3 Elementary Flying School, (EFTS) was commanded by Wing Commander Sir Robert Clark Hall, KBE, CMG, DSO, RAF (Ret'd) who was a retired Air Commodore and had volunteered to do what turned out to be a wonderful job as Station Commander, where he was extremely well liked.

The Station was so agreeably well run that it was sometimes known as 'Hotel Harewood'. It was the same alternate day, changing at midday, routine which we had become used to at Levin. Flying in the morning, ground school in the afternoon and next morning, then flying that afternoon and next morning again.

First day along with several other trainees, I met my instructor who wanted to know if I had flown and not content with a 'Yes', wanted to know how much. My private pilot's licence seemed to please him so there and then, having previously been issued with a Sidcot suit, helmet and gloves and flying boots, we were soon out on the field doing a pre-flight inspection on a yellow-painted Tiger Moth (DH 82). Mr Prior did a circuit then after we landed he invited me to try one and after two more, he said, 'We'll go in and you can do one for Flying Officer Brown, the Acting Flight Commander'. After 'doing' one for Mr Brown, he sent me off to do some solo. I was the only solo aircraft at Harewood on that day which was noted with surprise by the duty pilot in the watch tower.

While not having flown for eighteen months, I found the Tiger Moth rather easier to control than the DH 60G (Gipsy Moth), being heavier and having a steerable tail skid. Otherwise, apart from more instruments, there was not a lot of difference.

As the course progressed there were new manoeuvres to be learned such as stalling, spinning and forced landing practice. This latter exercise was often carried out in the vicinity of a practice forced landing field, near the Waimakariri River and on these occasions, the exercise could be carried on to a fairly realistic conclusion. The same applied to precautionary landing practice.

Aerobatics became another exercise together with spinning recovery and also starting the engine in flight, which latter tended to be exciting when the engine proved a bit stubborn to start. This was only practised dual anyway and I believe it was later eliminated from the syllabus.

Looking back, I realise all pupils were under pressure and indeed we all worked very hard and long to make the most of the course. One day during the progress of the course, my instructor, Pilot Officer Prior, took me aside and asked me how I felt about volunteering for Service Flying Training School in Canada. I replied that I would quite like to qualify for my wings in New Zealand. He then intimated to me that if I did not volunteer I would in all probability be kept back in New Zealand as a flying instructor. I let my name go forward for the Canadian course.

After the EFTS course ended, those of us who had opted for the Canadian course, were given some extra time at Harewood before leaving on our embarkation, or 'final' leave. One of my friends on the course, Mervyn de Clifford, lived at Riverton in Southland, where his widowed mother owned and ran the Wallace County Hotel. Mervyn very kindly invited me to spend some of my final leave down there which I greatly enjoyed. Mervyn was a died-in-the-wool fighter aspirant and he was very much looking forward to making the acquaintance of Spitfires and Hurricanes.

Our final leave was timed to expire at the wharf by the side of the *Awatea* berthed in Auckland. She was formerly on the trans Tasman Sydney–Auckland run from which it had been withdrawn mid-1940 to undertake wartime ferrying duties such as we were now about to commence.

The vessel was a fast liner of some 13,452 tons and carried 390 passengers and a crew of 237. At the time she was considered to be one of three fastest merchant ships in the world. There was a gold greyhound at the masthead normally, which indicated her record-breaking feats on the Tasman Sea.

We found that the ship had already embarked Australian U/T airmen in Sydney and our number would now make up the complement. Like the RAAF contingent we were all accommodated in cabins – the only obvious concession to wartime being an extra folding bed in a normally two-berth cabin. As we slid out of Auckland's Waitemata Harbour, in April 1941, we were joined by the cruiser HMS *Achilles* which took up station abreast of the *Awatea* as we proceeded north up the Pacific to Fiji (Suva).

Suva was the first foreign port I had visited and I was amazed at the greenness everywhere. We were all intrigued by the silverware being offered for sale by the Indian traders, the unusual foods and areas of general interest everywhere. Stepping back at one time, I felt something soft under my foot and when I turned round I found I had stepped on the bare toe of a very large Fijian policeman who smiled acceptance of my apology.

The day ashore sped by and we were on our way again in company with the *Achilles* and we resumed our detailed duties, standing by the big gun at the stern. There was a roster for this seemingly responsible but boring task and when we took up our position at the gun we called up on a marine telephone by the gun and a distorted voice acknowledged our presence. At other times we had the run of most of the ship. The meals were excellent with full steward service. There were all the deck games to be enjoyed as well as physical training of the service style, and lectures on Air Force subjects. The ship's cinema functioned at advertised times also.

We had been issued with tropical kit before we left Auckland so that dress had become the order of the day before reaching Fiji. The Australians had a very good style of tropical uniform and they too enjoyed the freedom which this type of gear provided.

About half way from Fiji to Vancouver, as far as we could judge, the *Achilles* bade us farewell by coming much closer alongside and passing a good luck message on the loud hailer and sounded their ship's whistle/horn.

They turned around and our guardian then became a Canadian Navy vessel called the *Prince Rupert*. This ship appeared to have been designed for quieter waters than we were now experiencing and her crew seemed to be taking a punishing time as the vessel wallowed mightily, especially compared with our own steady progress in the *Awatea*. The *Prince Rupert* bade us farewell also on loud speaker and ship's horn when we reached Victoria, British Colombia.

Disembarking at Victoria, we were marched up the main street in threes and after a brief interval, back again. The scenery as we approached the harbour and the city itself was magnificent and thoroughly enjoyed by all.

Back on board *Awatea*, the ship sailed on to Vancouver where we disembarked with all our kit straight onto a train of the Canadian Pacific Railway where we lived for the following few days. The accommodation consisted of long corridor coaches with double seats on each side of the aisle. These were adequate for four persons to sit on but they were at the disposal of two passengers facing each other, one on each. Meals were taken in the dining car with large panoramic windows enabling us to enjoy the magnificent scenery as we sped along. At night, a uniformed steward lowered the overhead bunk with its bedding in place and from it he retrieved the covers for the lower bed which was now contrived by sliding the two seats together. Now we had two comfortable full width beds for the two former occupants of the opposing seats. The steward completed the job by drawing curtains along the aisle to preserve privacy.

The train proceeded smoothly along, day and night, through the Rockies and out onto the prairie, only stopping occasionally to change engines and things like that. We found from experience that we preferred the oil-burning locomotives to the coal burners. The oilers being free of the soot and grittiness of the former, of course.

Arriving at Medicine Hat, in Alberta, we were transported to No. 34 SFTS and arrived at night in the middle of May 1941 to find an RAF station flying Harvards. My course mates and I had been recommended for multi-engined aircraft and so had been separated from the keen fighter types like my friend Mervyn de Clifford. We found out later that *they* had gone to a multi-engined training school where they were flying Cessna Cranes. Disappointment flourished all round.

However, in charge of us at Medicine Hat, was a young fresh faced

RAF administrative pilot officer who lost no time in addressing us in terms of admonishment about our deportment and the improvement he expected forthwith. His words were so well chosen in his English provincial accent that it had the desired effect and in no time the long barrack room with double bunks had been straightened up and not only made shipshape but was quiet as well.

It appeared that we were only there temporarily and we would be moving on to Moose Jaw. Any joy at the thought of the correct multi-engined posting were dispelled when we learned from the RAF trainees at Medicine Hat that Moose Jaw had Harvards too. More noise until the RNZAF liaison officer arrived and eventually explained that there had been a mix-up and the other part of the course had started training so we would just have to get on with it. Here, at Moose Jaw, we had another very efficient RAF administration pilot officer who saw to it that we did. We were now stationed at No. 3 SFTS, being the RAF Flying Training School at Moose Jaw.

Although it was May, the ground was still soft after the thaw and the station roads had still not been completed. Very sticky mud was in abundance. The parade ground was still being formed and the use of multi-tyred/wheeled rolling devices was a new item to most of us from New Zealand although common enough today throughout this country too.

As at Levin, Harewood and on the *Awatea* etc., I found I was again i/c, (in charge) of a half section of the course and the day was arranged in the time-tested way of half the course flying and half at ground school, alternating with the change taking place at mid-day each day.

My Flight Lieutenant instructor turned out to be an ex-operational Canadian of the same name as my EFTS instructor, Prior, in New Zealand. I later had a Norwegian Lieutenant Stene who was very pleasant also. He said to me one day, later in the course, 'I think you will be going onto multi-engined types because of your instrument flying technique.'

While at Levin and Harewood we learned about the old Vickers machine-gun and the Lewis gun. Now at Moose Jaw we had to become familiar with the Browning and the Vickers GO (gas operated) machine-guns and be examined on their operation.

Night flying was another new adventure undertaken at Moose Jaw. Because of the blackout and airfield lighting restrictions in England, our night flying practice took place with just the flare path to judge the approach by. The Airfield Control Pilot (ACP) gave us signals in the circuit and on the ground by Aldis lamp. There was no radio telephone at this stage—we replied to the ACP on the cockpit key, through the signal lamps on the aircraft. This was very basic night flying which was somewhat easier later when operating the Spitfire with glidepath indicators. (Louvred lamps pointing into the approach path which indicated green, when the approach path was satisfactory; red, when too low; and amber, when too high. The pilot to make adjustment accordingly). The Spitfire was very blind, with its long nose, when straight on to the flarepath. Later in the United Kingdom we also had a Chance Light, (floodlight), at the threshold of the runway, operated by the ACP if required.

The runways were often out of wind at Moose Jaw and this would tend to lead to a swing if a touchdown was made with drift. Here, the Harvard, on runways, had to be handled with care and to offset drift instant correction was required. Once, early on in my solo time, I was a bit late and I damaged the wing tip. That fortunately was the only time I damaged an aircraft in my flying career.

Cross-country navigation exercises were an enjoyable experience but with such flat featureless countryside round the base, a close attention to learned procedures and vigilance was necessary. One of our number set 'red on blue' (compass course 180° out) and ended up hundreds of miles away before he found an airfield on which to force-land. In keeping with his name, he was, thereafter, called Wrong Way Round.

At the end of the course, we were handed our wings informally and without ceremony. We had been interviewed previously by the RAF Station Commander, Group Captain James, who, in my case, was very interested in how I had spent my leisure time pre-war in view of my earlier hernia history disability. I told him about civilian flying, cycling and an enduring interest in all things associated with aviation.

We all graduated as Sergeants and had our wings and stripes sewn on before we left Moose Jaw, on leave, to report to Halifax at the end of it, for embarkation to the United Kingdom.

On reporting in Halifax, an RAF clerk requested 'the following to answer their names'. When my name was called, I joined the named group and at the end having ticked off all the names on his list, he said, 'You are all officers!' The delay was never explained. We had some time, before sailing, to take down our stripes which we had all had in common for our leave in Regina, Winnipeg, Toronto, Montreal and now at Halifax. Our quarters were now separate and also we were required to have our uniforms altered accordingly. Our modified airmans' uniforms would have to suffice for now and until we could order new ones in England.

Meanwhile we had learned that we, as a course, were scheduled to board the *Dominion Monarch*, of the New Zealand Shipping Company, which had travelled through the Panama Canal and up the East Coast of America to Halifax. On board were our old course mates from Levin and EFTS, (those who hadn't been left behind in New Zealand etc.,) who had now been kitted out in their uniforms and some were inclined to be variations on a theme!

In the convoy for the Atlantic crossing there were several other liners obviously carrying troops like the *Dominion Monarch*. One that stood out was the *Empress of Russia*, which had four funnels and being a coal burner, made a lot of smoke trying to keep up with the much more modern vessels like our *Awatea* and *Dominion Monarch*. It was said that the struggling captain was often in trouble for making so much smoke and we used to pity the poor stokers.

There was the usual stint, at sea, on the gun platform but unlike our journey across the Pacific with only a single warship escort we now had a multitude of naval vessels and some of these were busy dropping depth charges and dashing about at high speed on anti-submarine duty. Those of us who had been commissioned had been elevated to officers' quarters which, in fact, were probably, in the course of war-time austerity, now no more luxurious than those we had occupied on the *Awatea* as LACs.

The course for the *Dominion Monarch*, on arrival at the British Isles, took us into the Irish Sea and we entered the Mersey where we were greatly impressed, as we progressed to our Liverpool berth on 2 September 1941, by the number of wrecks on both sides of the river caused by the Axis bombing.

Off the ship we went straight onto an English train. They looked small after the large North American variety of train but proved to be very comfortable and smooth travelling. As we were looking through an open carriage window, at what we thought was our first 'short of food' Englishman, he began urgently raising both arms and within seconds we realised why! We were in a very smoky tunnel. On and on we went in this comfortable train until we arrived at Bournemouth, on the South coast where chartered buses took my party to the Anglo-Swiss hotel. We were soon to be addressed by another fresh-faced pilot officer, who also knew the score.

The Anglo-Swiss was still under its full civilian control so we settled in quickly, enjoying room service as much as we had done on the previous sea and train journeys. Our youthful pilot officer kept us in touch with what was going on and arranged for all of us to have a night vision test. At this test site we were arranged in a line on chairs and a series of WAAF girls attached clips to the rear of the collar of our uniforms. Each of us had a pad in front on a desk and a pencil with which to write or draw what we saw on the personal screen in the completely darkened room. There was a click every time anyone tried to get too close to the test and one of the girls would re-fasten him with the clip again. I thought I must fail as I drew the shapes I saw in the dark. However, when I recovered my flying log book, inside the cover was stamped – 'Night Vision: Exceptional'.

Another day, a bus trip was taken to Farnborough where we had a decompression test which I also passed successfully, although there were some failures. I do not know what happened to them. I supposed they were retained on low to medium level flying work.

At this stage I began to think that I stood a good chance of going onto night fighters and in fact one of my friends, 'Bill' Jameson did, being posted onto Defiants at East Fortune in Scotland. My friend was to prove a very successful night fighter too, winning a DSO and DFC in a very short time. However, in due course my posting arrived and I was on my way to No. 58 Fighter Operational Training Unit (OTU) at Grangemouth, Scotland, to train on Spitfires.

CHAPTER THREE

FIGHTER OPERATIONAL TRAINING UNIT AND NUMBER 66 SQUADRON

On our departure for Scotland from Bournemouth, the Railway Transport Officer, (RTO) handed me a nominal roll containing the names of seven officers and nineteen NCOs. Remarkably this document has survived the intervening fifty-three years and is reproduced at Annex b. As a newly commissioned pilot officer i/c the party I was inclined to take it very seriously in view of the dire penalties promised for any shortfalls of duty, as outlined on the papers.

It was then September 1941 and after reading the orders and other material provided, I was keen to check my complement when we arrived at Waterloo Railway Station. We were met there by the RTO who had motor transport, (MT) waiting to take us across London to King's Cross Station where we would entrain and depart for Grangemouth in Scotland.

To my horror, my check of numbers revealed that eight of my listed NCOs had vanished. I was an entirely new pilot officer, in London for the first time and in charge of this party! On referring my problem to the RTO he suggested accepting the transport to Kings Cross and initiating any further action there. (It wasn't his problem!)

To my immense relief after a miserable journey, for me, across London, we were met by the missing NCOs who had travelled by tube, with which they were familiar and said they thought they were doing the right thing.

I am glad to say our overnight journey to Edinburgh and then on to Grangemouth, went smoothly and without further incident.

The RAF MT took us from the rail to our sleeping quarters at a large house called Avondale, in the countryside, where the air force staff had allocated beds etc., and then the MT took us back to the airfield.

The airfield at Grangemouth had been a civilian terminal in pre-war days and had permanent runways and airport buildings with tower and observation lounge. The latter had become the Officers' Mess with an overall view of the airfield which enabled us to see what our contemporaries were making of flying the Spitfires and Masters with which No. 58 OTU was equipped.

We were addressed by the Chief Flying Instructor in welcome and the scope of the Spitfire course outlined. He mentioned the impending decompression test and the use of oxygen operation which it provided. Another tuition method introduced at this time was the carts or trolleys containing TR9 radio telephone sets. These trolleys, we found, were to be pushed around the perimeter track by us, wearing our helmets and fabric-type oxygen mask/microphones. Having previously been briefed on formation procedures with signals and commands, these were practised on the ground with the trolleys in response to the instructor's commands in the tower. The aim of saving air time practising these exercises was readily achieved.

The Chief Ground Instructor informed me that I was in charge of No. 12 course and would be responsible for them attending tuition periods at the times shown on the timetable which he provided.

The course consisted of numerous nationalities—there being a number of New Zealanders, like myself, Australians, Canadians, Jamaicans and Poles. Getting my tongue around some of the Polish names proved difficult at first.

We practised formation with the carts, also we learned about and were examined on the Spitfire. We had to be conversant with the hydraulic system and emergency measures to be taken with the undercarriage, the oxygen system and of course all the operating temperatures and pressures as appropriate.

Meanwhile, leading up to flying solo, in the Spitfires, we had been receiving dual practice on the Miles Master I aircraft in simulated Spitfire circuits which entailed using reduced flap and maintaining a curved approach onto the runway. This latter allowed visibility past the long nose of the Spitfire. Having satisfied the instructors in the air and on the ground, that we were conversant with handling the Spitfire IA, we were sent off solo.

Flying the Spitfire was a very unique and enjoyable experience and all so entirely new. We had practised formation flying at SFTS but here it required more practice with a clean fast aircraft. Tail chasing and dog fighting were fun.

Aerobatics brought new delights but I remember an early loop when I discovered in the initial acceleration, the ailerons appeared to be frozen. After several experiments I asked the instructor about it. He said, simply, 'the fabric ailerons of the Mark I. The metal ailerons require more care as they are much more sensitive and you will experience them as the course progresses.'

We were flying Mark IA Spitfires at Grangemouth and some of these, as well as having fabric-covered ailerons, were equipped with hand-pumped undercarriages the pump lever was located on the right-hand side of the cockpit. The aircraft thus equipped could be recognised sometimes downwind, because when a pilot changed hands to pump, he tended to also pump the stick with his left hand in sympathy, which, transmitted to the elevators, gave a slight rocking motion.

Eventually we were introduced to air-to-air firing at the drogue towed by one of the Station's Fairey Battles. The officer in charge of this programme briefed us on the perils of practising with live ammunition. The bullets were dipped in paint so that each individual mark on the drogue would be recognised and scored accordingly. He added, somewhat menacingly, that every mark on the Battle would cost the pilot who fired it one pound (Sterling). A lot of money in those days.

The Battle crew were very aware of their vulnerability and would not tolerate any attack approach which decreased from the beam to within 45° or so of the stern. An unmistakable and almost frenzied 'Back off, Back off!', on the TR9 radio was the result if we inadvertently reduced the angle of attack below 45°.

On these exercises only two guns were armed, of the eight Brownings in the wings. A camera gun recorded the attack technique of each pupil and these were viewed and assessed later by the armament instructors.

Our course had not been without its casualties. Being now September, in Scotland the mists were increasing and there was a lot of high ground around the airfield to snare the unfortunate pupil flying an aircraft with which he was yet to become familiar, in poor visibility. The radio telephone in the form of the TR9 was limited in range, especially low down, when trying to return to base under cloud. Several pupils found the high ground and I lost two very good friends in this manner. Others on the course took to authorised low flying too literally and one tried to fly through a brick house!

The flaps and brakes on the Spitfire both rely on compressed air for operation and when the air supply fails both those services are lost together. Landing without flaps becomes a high speed affair also without brakes after touchdown which ended in one pupil silently creeping up on an airfield working party, with disastrous results for the working party.

At the end of the six weeks' course there was a 'dining-in-night' with all the conventions of passing the wine and the loyal toast etc. With all that formality concluded, the Chief Instructor, (CI) gave a fairly traditional speech which included, 'Never have so many Spitfires been broken by so few'. At the conclusion of the CI's oration, Mr Vice stood up an announced, 'I will now call on Pilot Officer Coldbeck to reply'. I was astonished! I had been enjoying myself until that moment. However, I stood up and said something like, 'Mr President, I can't thank the CI for his unkind remarks but we're doing our best and we hope, in due course, that we will bring credit to Grangemouth and our future squadrons'. I sat down amidst thunderous applause, for nothing at all. This speech-making was the latest in a line of shocks of extra responsibilities I had received at each stage of training.

The 'dining-in' had signalled the end of our stay at Grangemouth and we were no longer a course and so were despatched independently to our various postings. Myself and two others from New Zealand, Matheson and Wyn Meares, were posted to No. 66 Squadron and someone had looked up the appropriate secret book and found it to be at Angle, in South Wales.

After lots of changes of trains, we arrived in Wales from Scotland, and eventually the small town of Angle and finally the Royal Air Force Station of the same name. Passing along one of the streets in the town, the three of us in RAF uniform must have inadvertently provoked an old woman into berating us angrily, in the Welsh dialect.

The Squadron Commander of the Station's only Squadron, welcomed us warmly but had to tell us that his was the only Squadron at Angle and he was expecting to be operating Havocs. Someone made some more investigations and found that 66 Squadron was at Perranporth in Cornwall. So having inspected the rubberised runways which were new to us, we set off again, this time for Perranporth.

On the train overnight, various service personnel proffered advice about Cornwall—where to go, what to see, including the best pubs such as the Red Lion in Truro—and so on. Perranporth sent transport to meet us at Truro where we left the train and this time we were at the right place, finding 66 Squadron to be the only Squadron at Perranporth where they were flying Spitfire IIAs, modified with a 30-gallon tank permanently fixed to the port wing.

We found that the Squadron sleeping quarters were in the Droskyn Castle Hotel which was still operating in its civilian capacity. The hotel enjoyed a breathtaking view down a magnificent beach which was out of bounds due to it being obstructed as an anti-invasion precaution. We just slept there, being transported to and from the airfield in various RAF runabout canvas-covered vehicles. The food up on the airfield was very good indeed and thoroughly enjoyed by all. We had such luxuries as strawberries and cream, eggs and other delightful country food.

The Squadron Commander, Squadron Leader 'Dizzy' Allen, DFC, a Battle of Britain pilot, welcomed us and next day we began familiarisation with the Mark IIA Spitfire. The most obvious difference from the Mark I being the rather ugly appendage of the 30-gallon tank and the Koffman Starter. Regarding the latter; engine starting involved priming the motor and setting the throttle and switching on the ignition. Pressing a starter button fired a cartridge and most times the engine started. Sometimes the engine did not start and after going through the five cartridges in the magazine, the pilot discovered the ignition still turned off! Red faces all round especially the NCO I/C, but his for a different reason, he being responsible for rearming the plane's starter magazine. With the increased weight of the new tank and drag on the port side, we were behove to open up slowly to obtain slip-stream over the tail and thus, directional control. Everything in the top right-hand corner!

In the excitement of a 'scramble' to undertake a potential interception, many an aircraft went into an uncontrolled swing to the left. In this connection, one day when the Air Officer Commanding (AOC), was visiting, there was the alarming sight of three tarpaulin-covered wrecks on the airfield. I believe eventually there was an order out to leave the extra tank empty. I understood the original purpose of the tank was to give the Spitfire extra range when escorting the Blenheim bombers to carry out raids on the two German Pocket Battleships, *Scharnhorst* and *Gneisenau* in Brest harbour. Often, unfortunately, the Blenheims we were to escort were late and the extra fuel carried in the clumsy 30-gallon tank on the port wing, had been used up before setting course. On one such operation there were twelve of us flying Spitfire IIAs in a squadron block of four threes in 'V' formation. I had been allocated the position in the middle of the formation directly astern of the Squadron Leader (Duckenfield). With a Spitfire formating on each of my wings—i.e. the CO in front of me, a Spitfire on each wing and the centre man of the rearward three directly behind me, in line astern with his two wing men. As was usual, in those days, in close formation all were concentrating on keeping station and navigation was in the hands of the leader. So, focusing on keeping my position, I was horrified to feel the throttle handle grow loose in my grip. Just to test what I guessed must be the case, I lifted my closed left hand and the throttle lever came with it. Stuck now with a low boost setting, I began immediately to fall back and the gap between my three and the one in front began to widen. The only thing I could think to do was to gently lower the nose, pick up speed and, so as to ensure anyone still following would know not to follow, I transmitted 'leaving formation'.

Having dived clear, I levelled off and turned North. There was only sea and cloud to be seen but I imagined that as we were ostensibly heading for Brest, I must be heading back across the English Channel. I changed R/T channel to the advised frequency and after a while, requested a homing. The reply was that I should climb, for safety, to which I replied that I was unable to climb owing to my low power setting. They gave me my heading for base and meanwhile by dint of much blind feeling and groping down the side of the cockpit, I located the rod connected to the throttle, which I left as it was until I was in a good position to land, should I happen to close the throttle and could not open it again. When I did land, all the ground crew came out with question marks over their heads and one was trying to marshal me into a parking bay but I had to switch off on the perimeter track. I threw the throttle handle to the NCO i/c who caught it neatly.

The Spitfire throttle lever was an elegant ivory-handled affair with THROTTLE engraved in red along the handle. The lever which descended out of sight into the throttle box was composed of two pieces end-butted together and joined by another piece held in place with, (from memory), six screws, three each side of the butted joint. The added piece acted as a hinge when the pilot was required to move the lever through the gate. The so-called 'hinge' had broken along the line of the screws.

I retrieved the throttle with its ivory handle and red engraved THROTTLE and I was permitted to keep it in my kit. Unfortunately, it disappeared from my belongings, at base, along with my two cameras and *all* my photographs, both personal and service ones too, when I was later shot down off Augusta in Sicily.

To continue with the story of early Squadron life on 66, at Perranporth, in 1941, my Flight Commander was Flight Lieutenant Collingridge and he detailed Wyn Meares and me to fly No. 2 to various experienced operational pilots for formation practice at first then onto convoy patrols. These patrols were a simple operation of flying out to the Cornish coast where a convoy was proceeding and communicating with the Master-in-charge of the convoy after which we would fly around it in long line astern without flying over the convoy. We flew for about an hour then formed up again on recall to base.

I well remember on Christmas Day 1941, before a festive lunch, flying one of these patrols with my great friend Laddie Lucas. He had recently been appointed Flight Commander. As well as a flight commander change, we had a new squadron commander when Squadron Leader Duckenfield took over from 'Dizzy' Allen. Wyn Meares departed, on posting, for 79 Squadron at Baginton and a Hurricane conversion. A couple of us visited him there in the deep snow, among all the depressed-looking Whitleys.

Our weather in winter at Perranporth was very much better than elsewhere in the UK and so it was at Portreath, further down the coast. We were sent off about once a month on operational leave, given a rail warrant and a tacit invitation to 'get lost' for ten days. Those of us from the Antipodes, for want of anything better in winter quite often found our way to London where there were all sorts of exciting things to do and see. There were cheap hostels for officers, like the Salvation Army Red Shield in Paddington, plain but suitable for our limited resources. Returning from one of these operational junketings, we asked the MT driver who met us at the railway station for any news and he said, 'Not much, just 66 Squadron has moved'. What?! Panic subsided when we discovered they had just moved to Portreath, down the coast.

From being the only Squadron on the station, we now had all sorts of other air force units and aircraft to keep us company. We also discovered that the OC Flying Wing was a New Zealand officer in the RAF, Wing Commander 'Mindy' Blake, DSO, DFC, who was using a Curtiss P-40 as his personal hack.

There was the Walrus amphibian and its operator who never did take us on a promised fishing trip in it, probably off the coast of Cornwall, mainly because of the wintry sea conditions and service commitments. Arriving home from 'Operational leave', to find the Squadron had moved from Perranporth to Portreath, I suppose spared us all the packing up and movement orders etc., but being of an age when such things were taken in one's stride, it was hardly noticed.

Portreath was a much busier flying station; being the home of the Overseas Aircraft Despatch Unit (OADU), there being always a good supply of aircraft for the enthusiast, such as I was, to look at. Nearly all the aircraft to be seen there had been pictured in New Zealand, but few actually seen in life or flight. The Armstrong Whitworth Ensign, a very large graceful-looking tail wheel undercarriage four-engined airliner, was one visitor which had always attracted my admiration, until I saw it flying when it appeared to be hanging in the sky. An American Curtiss Wright 20, which was a large-bodied twin-engined aircraft with a tail wheel undercarriage, was an interesting visitor; and later, in 1942, I remember the despatch officer at Luqa, in Malta, asking me if I knew what the Curtiss Wright 20 looked like, I was thus able to tell him. Apparently what made it popular on the Malta run was its ability to carry a very good payload as well as not needing a great deal of refuelling for the return flight to Gibraltar. Bisleys, Blenheims, Beaufighters, Beauforts, Wellingtons and even Whitleys were commonplace at Portreath with the occasional fast twins like the DH Mosquito and Westland Whirlwind.

On the Squadron at Portreath the same routine as practised at Perranporth was largely the order of the day, and night. Night-flying and night cross-countrys were practised and because in the main, the weather was clear, most were enjoyable. We had the use of glide path indicators set for the Spitfires which made the approach much easier – and safer.

Laddie Lucas, as our Flight Commander with Raoul Daddo-Langlois as his deputy, ensured the flight ran smoothly and pleasantly for all its members. Sometimes an evening out would be organised by Laddie after flying had finished and we had been stood down. These took the form of a dinner at one of the very good hotels which were situated at St Ives, Truro, Redruth and Newquay. A bottle of wine would be shared at dinner and the return to base made at a reasonable hour. These were very good hotels with a very fine standard of cuisine although it was wartime. Whilst at Portreath, we slept at one of the commandeered houses down on the flat behind the harbour. These were houses with quite large bedrooms and high ceilings where several pilots using each room was not over-crowding. There were two routes from the flat area to the airfield which we took in service transport. One, the more circuitous, was via the cliff top, with its great views of the sea down below. The other route was somewhat steeper and more direct, up from the village and through the woods. Our Mess was up on the Station where we arrived for breakfast and took other meals and unless we were on an evening out with the Flight, dinner too.

Daily, on the airfield, there was the standard 'at readiness' where we would sit in the crew-room, with Mae West, (life-jacket) and flying boots on. The parachute with helmet were at the aircraft, ready to be donned in a flash after running there, on the signal. When not on duty at any of the various states of readiness, we could be excused to carry out any of our personal messages or activities. A favourite diversion of mine as the occasion arose, was to check out some of the transit aircraft in the OADU. One which I saw and which was not attached to OADU, was a Spitfire without the usual camouflage, but painted all over in a medium blue colour. I asked my mentor, Raoul Daddo-Langlois, about it. He explained by saying, 'That is a PRU Spitfire', and to my further questions, went on to say that they were specially equipped and un-armed to carry out long solo sorties into enemy territory to photograph targets and also the result of raids on targets. He added that the pilots were all volunteers. This was my introduction to this type of aerial operations which interested me.

Life continued in the Flight, relieved now and again by an interception patrol (IP), which was initially exciting enough but that soon wore off because we never saw anything! One day, Pilot Officer Mann, Squadron Adjutant, asked around to see if anyone would like to volunteer for a PRU posting which had come in. I had been thinking about what Raoul had told me and in the end I put my name forward.

I was pretty sure there would be a course to fit me for such a different role and I looked forward to hearing about it. That was to prove a disappointment. The Squadron Commander's comment when he found out about my volunteering, was that I needed my head read and did I not know that I had to fly my aircraft to the Middle East? I did not. The CO wished me luck and in a few days, having said goodbye to my very good friends on 66 Squadron, I was on my way to a funny little grass airfield called Detling, in Kent. There was no flying taking place during my time there, with the cloud base almost within touching distance and the visibility hardly to the boundary fence. A number of other pilots had gathered, for what we anticipated would be a Course. We were all billeted with families locally, which was a new and novel experience. I was glad when it was over.

Our daytime was spent shivering in an intensely cold Nissen hut, with a little coke stove, as a token gesture against the freezing cold. It was a most inadequate gesture and I have not forgotten that cold!

With chattering teeth we listened to the theory of camera operation and some advice on how to, in theory, avoid making vapour trails, a sure giveaway to the enemy while on photographic reconnaissance

(PR). Some of the rather varied members of the lecturer's audience were expressing disillusionment and dark remarks about recourse to applying for a change back. Some of these chaps had an equally motley collection of motor transport, which was not being improved out in the mid-winter snows. I do not know what happened to some of these PRU aspirants but some failed the decompression test, which we had taken again and others I knew found it possible to withdraw. Those few who were left were, after a few days, posted to RAF Benson (home of Photo Reconnaissance), where a Canadian Wing Commander assumed casual control of us. Daily flying activity was called for in the form of picking up PR Spitfires from various Maintenance Units (MU) around the country. We were detailed to travel to these MUs as passengers in an old Anson, piloted by a Commonwealth flight sergeant whose navigation methods gave us some real cause for concern.

On take-off, the Flight Sergeant would acknowledge our presence by signalling us to wind the undercarriage up, which required multiple turns on a wheel adjacent to his seat. He would then turn his compass grid ring until he found out which way we were heading and set his direction indicator accordingly. He then attempted to relate our heading to the map he was trying to read, on his knee, and of course it was not long before we were signalled by the Flight Sergeant to lower the undercarriage again because he intended landing at that airfield which had fortunately appeared below. Having successfully landed, one of us was invited to run into the Duty Pilot and find out where we were! Back in the aircraft, most of us were trying to keep out of sight and distance ourselves from this navigational technique. After a search on the map, we again set off with only one more stop of that sort, before we reached Speke (Liverpool). I collected the Spitfire which was waiting for me and I returned to Benson in it in a more normal fashion.

Another time, the pick-up point for the Spitfire I was collecting, was Hendon and on the way there, barrage balloons began sailing past the windows of the Anson. In fact we were flying through the balloons in the barrage at Slough. Our protests, from our rearward seats, persuaded the same Flight Sergeant to put the Anson in a steeply banked turn and fortunately we escaped unharmed but demoralised. Upon reaching RAF Hendon, I thankfully found the Spitfire and made another uneventful return to Benson.

While at Benson, there was no particular emphasis on navigation or aerial photography. Our tutor at Detling had talked about handling the aircraft over the target but it seemed to be largely a matter of trial and error. The Wing Commander, on my initiative, authorised me a couple of long navigation sorties, at height, up the mainland to Scotland. On those, I practised turning onto targets of my own choosing. Navigation was, in this style of operation, in my view, a matter of adequate pre-flight preparation and constant vigilance to give oneself the best odds of survival.

It seemed that it was now only a matter of time before my aircraft, which I was to fly to the Middle East, would come up, so I busied myself with a set of maps, obtained from the Intelligence Section, covering a route, via Gibraltar and Malta, terminating at Cairo. The Wing Commander had authorised me to draw a Dalton Computer which was in the form of a knee pad containing a roller blind under an Azimuth ring on which course to steer could be worked out against wind speed etc. On the cover was an Appleyard scale and a pad for noting courses and target details.

As one of the most useful acknowledgements, regarding this somewhat cavalier pioneering detail to fly to the Middle East, the Wing Commander arranged for the sole survivor of a two aircraft detachment to Gibraltar, to give three of us who went to Benson, a talk on transporting ourselves to the Middle East. This officer began by stating that he could not talk about beyond Gibraltar to the Middle East, only the route to Gibraltar and back again as he had not been beyond Gibraltar.

Coming back from Gibraltar, the two of them had left about the same time but our lecturer had experienced very strong headwinds and only managed to force-land out of fuel on the South Coast of England. Unfortunately the other pilot was not heard of again.

On the route down to Gibraltar, the lecturer strongly advised getting the Met. Office to give an assurance that the North Coast of Spain would be in clear before setting off. Otherwise, 'Don't go', If on the estimated time of arrival, there was no sign of the North Coast of Spain – 'come back!'. Three or four pilots were waiting about at Benson for duties about which I was not sure but three or four days into my stay, I was having my breakfast when an airman messenger rushed in and stated that the Wing Commander had detailed me to take off in Spitfire AB 300 at once and head for Portreath, as the weather was closing in. I tore up to my room, in the Mess, slammed the lid on my trunk, having packed it each night, and picked up my parachute bag, in which I had my essentials for potential overnight stops, to place on top of the cameras in the fuselage of AB 300. I gave the batman a couple of pounds to arrange to have my trunk taken to the equipment section and shipped to the

Middle East. Some three years later I found that he had done exactly as I requested.

I took off from Benson and set off for Portreath where I found the weather was still reasonable. I reported to Overseas Aircraft Despatch Unit, (OADU) where the Squadron Leader in charge asked me where I was going. To my reply, 'To the ME' he said he hadn't had one of you chaps through previously, and anyway, you can look after yourself can't you?' So I said, 'Yes', and thanked him!

When I surfaced each following morning there were Bisleys, Blenheims and Wellingtons still parked on the airfield, waiting to go to the ME. They were supposed to depart before daylight so I decided if they can't go, neither can I and Met. confirmed 'No north coast of Spain clear.' During my wait, at this time, I had told the ground staff Sergeant, when he enquired, that I thought AB 300 was running a bit rough and he said he would look at it. After a few test flights and waiting three days, I rose to find none of the transit fleet in sight and after a check with the Met. Office I again tore round, paid my Mess bill, jumped into AB 300 and took off for Gibraltar.

I was quite a long way into my first leg, across the Bay of Biscay, from Cornwall, when base called me up on the VHF. Since I had previously been scolded for breaking radio silence in the Bay I didn't answer at first, however as the calls kept coming with continuing urgency I eventually replied, looking over my shoulder in case someone was homing in on me. HQ then requested a tuning transmission which I gave. They replied that they thought I was off course, but in the event all was well. On I went at 25,000 feet at about 310 TAS (true air speed). To my great relief, the north coast of Spain was clear to see. However, to the south was a complete cover of cloud. Notwithstanding, I carried on and the cloud sheet began to break up further south so that I was able to identify Lisbon. I confidently continued on to the Straits of Gibraltar and Gibraltar itself.

At Gibraltar in those days there was a special procedure for joining the circuit. Aircraft had to fly south of the Rock in the Straits then turn north, lower the undercarriage and fire the colours of the day. Being aware of this routine before departure from Portreath, I had loaded the aircraft Very pistol with the appropriate cartridge. In the PR Mark IV, unlike some later Marks, the pistol had to be withdrawn from its holster on the right-hand lower side of the cockpit and fired out of a previously opened canopy, while being held in front of the face. Having accomplished this satisfactorily, you looked towards the signal station on the Rock and hopefully received a green signal as permission to join the circuit around the Rock and land. The time now being a little after noonday, the flight had taken approximately three and a half hours. I received a Green.

Unlike the briefing officer at Portreath, a Wing Commander at Gibraltar had decided he would dictate my movements and that he had decreed I would be flying the Wellington Route to Malta, at 10,000 feet, which he proceeded to show me! I was horrified! He thus demonstrated that he knew nothing of my aircraft, its performance or mine. The route to the middle of the Mediterranean and height of 10,000 feet, was quite unsuitable for a Spitfire and I came to the conclusion that it would be disastrous at that height on that route, so I prepared two flight plans – one for the Wellington and one that took me to Malta at 25,000 feet.

I spent the next day on navigation planning and my aircraft and a quick shopping trip into the town and sightseeing. First thing next morning I asked the Sergeant to have AB 300 fuelled up and wheeled out. There was no sign of the aforementioned Wing Commander so I took off for Malta and climbed to my cruising altitude of 25,000 feet. There was later some high cloud but I stayed in visual contact with the ground and and descended to 18,000 feet to negotiate the Atlas Mountains. Passing the Gulf of Hammamet, I was amazed at the wonderful visibility which enabled me to see a snow-covered Mount Etna, in Sicily, emerging. Recognising such islands as Pantellaria, Linosa and Lampedusa, I eventually announced my arrival to Control at Malta. The Controller there directed me not to land at my flight plan destination, (Luqa) because of low flying enemy aircraft in the circuit but to land at the Northern Airfield, which of course was Takali.

CHAPTER FOUR

MALTA – EARLY DAYS – 1942

Landing at the Northern Malta airfield, (Takali), I found the two smiling figures welcoming me, to be Laddie Lucas and Raoul Daddo-Langlois. I had been puzzled, at Portreath, at the lack of any evidence of 66 Squadron – they were away somewhere, was the only explanation I could unearth from airfield personnel. It appears, Laddie and Raoul had travelled as passengers out to Malta, alighting at Kalafrana in a Sunderland flying boat, in anticipation of flying the first Spitfires which had been flown off the carrier a few days previously. Raoul accused me – tongue in cheek – when observing my landing at Takali, of 'dropping' AB 300. (An exaggerated term for a landing which might have been a trifle high).

There were several others from 66 Squadron in evidence there which made it something of a reunion, before I began the third leg of my journey to the Middle East. I wallowed in the warmth of my welcome. They accused me of 'shooting a line', when in reply to a question, I said I had had to come down to 18,000 feet to stay in contact near the Atlas Mountains.

I reported to the Intelligence Section at Takali who seemed to be the main purveyors to me of news and/or orders. A very pleasant Flight Lieutenant took me under his wing and guided me up to the Mess at M'dina, which was a fine building up on an escarpment overlooking the Takali airfield. The building in which the Mess was situated had a long balcony from which one had not only a commanding view of Takali airfield but right down the Island to Luqa and beyond – at this time being heavily bombed.

I had been watching with something akin to horror as the Ju 88s dived on Luqa, pounding the airfield with their bombs. The orange flames and flashes with attendant smoke and dust must have been making life pretty miserable down there. My guide, the Intelligence officer (IO), said to me a while later, 'You won't be pleased to hear this, but you're staying here!' I thought he meant by staying here that I should be staying at Takali rather going on to Luqa as planned

47

to prepare for my departure to the ME – but no, it was Malta, not Takali, he meant, by 'here'.

Next day, Luqa remaining my destination, I started up AB 300 and flew it down there. On arrival at Luqa I was very interested in all that was going on among the bomb damage and wreckage and enjoyed another welcome from new Service acquaintances on the airfield. I was informed by the Luqa Station Headquarter's Staff, (SHQ) that I would be attached to 69 Squadron for all purposes and this was confirmed by teleprinter. Everyone on the airfield appeared, with good reason, to be wearing tin hats. I hadn't brought mine because of the bulk and weight in the Spitfire and in consequence, I didn't have one for my entire time on Malta, or for that matter, the rest of the war. All available tin helmets had been issued from Malta Stores. Ground crews had preference. Later, I was taken by a service driver in a little Fiat Topolina, with my small kit in a parachute bag, and shown where I was allocated a room at Siggiewi Signal Station which I found was about half an hour's walk over, on the far side of the airfield. I slept there for the whole of my time on Malta.

I was introduced to nobody on 69 Squadron but eventually I located the Squadron Commander, Wing Commander Tennant. He shrugged and said, 'I know nothing about PRU, you will have to look after yourself'. Later, I was approached by a pilot on the airfield, one 'Johnnie' Walker and another pilot, Flt Lt Kelly, who had 'landed' recently at Luqa in one of two Mosquitoes. The pilot of the other, I was told, had feathered one engine which had been overheating, but when he tried to land with one feathered, he appeared to have reached his critical speed and spun in. The resulting matchwood determined the write-off category of that Mosquito and put the navigator in hospital.

'Johnnie' Walker's aircraft was bombed after it landed and was at that time, again under repair. This repair and bombing alternately had effectively kept it on the ground. Both pilots expressed a strong desire to fly AB 300. I replied that I didn't have authority to let anyone else fly it on a casual basis. They came back a day later with authority from Air HQ to fly the Spitfire so 'Johnnie' Walker signed up the 700, the Air Force Serviceability form, and was away about an hour and came back OK. The other pilot had a flight of similar duration and that was the last I heard from them about flying 'my' aircraft. They didn't explain about where they actually went or what they did.

A day or so later, 13 March 1942, as I was standing outside the Intelligence Office on the gravel, Flt Lt Kerridge, the Chief Intelligence Officer at Luqa, emerged and approached me with a thin strip of teleprinter paper in his hand and said, 'Coldbeck, I have a "Form Green" here which requires a 69 Squadron PRU Spitfire to photograph certain Sicilian airfields'. I thought to myself, so that is a Form Green. For a Spitfire to take photographs it needed a pilot and as I was standing there with no one else in sight apparently qualified to fly it. I accepted the 'Form Green' which the Officer proferred and after preparing myself, by locating my targets on the map I had acquired and the aircraft being full and serviceable, off I went. I had enquired about airfield procedure, which wasn't very formal owing to the conditions obtaining.

I think it was 'Johnnie' Walker who had said to me in conversation, that it would not be a good idea to climb to operating height straight over Sicily. I hope it would have occurred to me anyway, with Sicily only 60 miles away. I therefore went away from Malta on 070° over the sea to about 12,000 feet then on up to 25,000 feet on my second leg, on the way to the East Coast of Sicily – Mt Etna, snow-covered, in the clear air, that day, provided a great pivot to swing around. Over Catania airfield, at the foot of Mt Etna, I was startled by the black puffs which appeared alongside and behind me after a slight noise belatedly awakened me to their presence. This unwelcome attention of the heavy anti-aircraft fire continued right across Catania and over Gerbini as well, as I photographed the airfields with hundreds of aircraft down there. To photograph Catania I flew slightly to one side until I found I was almost level then made a steep turn over the field turning the cameras on as I went. I turned the cameras off when I thought I would have covered it. Another steep turn to check. The control of the cameras during a photo run was through a grey metal box which was located under the windscreen where the reflector sight is located in a fighter Spitfire. Two knobs controlled exposure interval rate and start and finish respectively. Another window on the box showed the number of exposures made.

The aircraft I was flying on this day, 13 March 1942, was of course the only Photo Reconnaissance (PR) Spitfire on Malta at this time. AB 300 which type was known at one time as a Spitfire Mark V 'D' type but eventually became universally accepted as the PR Mark IV, powered by the Rolls-Royce Merlin 45 with a de Havilland metal three-bladed constant speed airscrew. The Spitfire in this form was constructed with specially designed wings of the same plan form as a Mark V fighter Spitfire but containing no armament or fittings for guns of any sort, and with leading edge tanks of 66 gallons capacity right along from wing root to tip each side. This leading edge tankage was in addition to two main central Spitfire fuselage self-sealing tanks which contained 86 gallons in total. A grand all-up total of 218 gallons.

In managing the fuel it was usual for the pilot to take off with all or mains on then when airborne on the climb, to turn off main tanks and continue on the wing tanks only. If the main tanks were left turned on the engine would feed from them until exhausted therefore it behove the pilot to conserve those central self-sealing tanks until last or for an emergency. This wing tankage absolutely precluded the installation of armament which has been erroneously mentioned by some writers in their enthusiasm for the PR pilots of their choice. This is not to say that all PR Spitfires were equipped in the same way but in my time on Malta, until November 1942, all PR Mark IV Spitfires, aggregating seven or eight in my flight, were of the same unarmed design – no guns installed or possible.

In keeping with Mark V variant Spitfires, the Merlin 45 used about 38 gallons an hour which of course depended on how hard the engine was used. It would use more if the pilot selected high engine revolutions on his cockpit control and it was more economical if operational requirements would allow low revolutions to be selected on the constant speed de Havilland airscrew. The oil and oxygen requirements had been suitably provided with capacity for the extended flying times of photographic reconnaissance aircraft.

Approaching Luqa after this, my first PR operational sortie, there was little activity, either friendly or enemy but I thought it was a mistake to continue using the same ancient call sign I had been given and mentioned this to the IO for an opinion. It was, a short time later, changed without further ado. (Call signs in the UK were often changed which I understood was to avoid the enemy identification of aircraft and activity). Anyway, I had photographed Catania and Gerbini then made my way to the Italian Naval and Seaplane base of Augusta further south on the east coast taking one hour 50 minutes flying time. On landing this first time I found the camera crew were first on the scene, busy un-loading the camera magazines from the tops of the cameras in the rear fuselage and thrusting a Pilot's report form at me to be filled in on the wingtip, using it as a desk. The fitter, rigger, and the camera crew were followed by instrument tradesman, (for changing oxygen bottles, the pilot had to be out of his seat before the oxygen system could be serviced. The armour plating behind the seat had to be moved forward.) The radio man was not far behind and then I made my way to the Intelligence Section which had been my starting point with Flight Lieutenant Kerridge, where they required all details of height and locations of photos as well as all other relevant aspects. The IO then obtained the Met. man on the phone and handed me over to him for further interrogation by him about cloud types and weather encountered. All this was interestingly novel to me at this stage.

Between the time of my AB 300 landing, on transfer, from Takali at Luqa and the operational sortie I had just completed, it seemed as though 'looking after myself' meant I belonged to one's self, so covetously, as I resumed standing around, I saw a *very* small room in the intelligence building with nothing in it. It had a window for light and a tall steel locker but nothing else. I dusted off a bombed table from a wrecked office and found an office chair and there was an armchair, in another wrecked section, which I found room for and squeezed in somehow.

There was no authorisation book available for me to enter my flights so I acquired a hard covered notebook of the same size from the SHQ which I ruled up with exactly the same columns and headings as an authorisation book and this book was in use for our PRU the whole of my eight months time of duty on Malta, at Luqa in 1942.

I do not know what 69 Squadron was doing at this time although I was nominally attached to them. There was not much flying activity going on with their Marylands. I saw one taxying past occasionally. I led a solitary life. I had not located their activity area. I met the 69 CO, Wing Commander Tennant again in passing, from time to time and at the month's end I put my log book into the Intelligence Office for signing by him. I supposed he had an office somewhere and perhaps a crewroom too. Mostly Wing Commander Tennant and I had a conversation limited to,

'You OK?'

'Yes, thanks Sir, – OK'.

My main associates were the Intelligence staff.

The Sergeant i/c Servicing, who looked after AB 300, through his small staff and also the Engineering Officer, would report on the serviceability now and again, as they now knew where to find me. After every bombing raid I would walk down to the little old dilapidated shed/hangar where they had put AB 300. At the end of my walk down there I would see if it had been damaged at all and have a chat with the ground crew who would be in the vicinity – great lads, under the command of the engineering officer out there on the open airfield. I continued to absorb the Form Greens addressed to 69 Squadron. They were delivered to me by the Intelligence Officer and were pieces of teleprinter paper which simply stated one PRU Spitfire to Photo Recce. A list of targets and the dates would follow. No times at this stage were stated. I took off when I considered it appropriate according to serviceabilty of AB 300 and the enemy aircraft in the vicinity. Another trip to Sicily followed on 15 March when, in addition to Catania and Gerbini, with heavy flak at those densely populated airfields, there was the more Western airfield of Castel Vetrano and also Bo Rizzo to be covered. Later in March there were sorties to other, (new to me), areas of Reggio Calabria, Messina and Palermo. Messerschmitt 109s began to manoeuvre for an interception at Palermo but I saw them before they became dangerous and made my escape out to sea, after photography. For the solo pilot, alone over enemy territory, eternal vigilance was the price of survival.

I covered all the Sicilian airfields several times in April then after Les Colquhoun arrived that month I took it for granted we had two aeroplanes to use and at my suggestion and in the absence of any orders or instructions, we took the Form Green orders in rotation and flew whichever aircraft was available. This was, incidentally, after all the new fighter Spitfires on Malta had either been shot down or otherwise made unserviceable on the ground, by enemy action. At the time, we two were the only aircraft airborne in daylight, so if we were within sight of each other on the ground we then knew the aircraft noise we were hearing approaching was the enemy. They had air superiority! We managed to sneak in and out when they were not looking and with the connivance of fighter control.

We on the airfield were all dodging bomb blasts, strafing attacks and falling shrapnel and masonry meanwhile. The Sergeant would bring the Form 700 for me to sign prior to one of my sorties. As flying personnel know, the Form 700 had columns for each of the tradesmen to sign up for their daily and other inspections including fuel and oil, oxygen etc. There were also details of hours flown so that minor and major inspections could be carried out at the proper time in the life cycle of the aircraft.

Eventually, AB 300 was the first and possibly the only Spitfire in 1942 to receive a major inspection on the Island. When the inspection came due I was casually informed the 'major' included an engine change. It had been going very well up to this point and appeared to lead a charmed life with only minor damage from time to time. One slight damage it received from a close-shave bomb, was to the canopy and as a result, because the canopy wouldn't stay on the aircraft, the Group Captain Station Commander came along to see for himself why it was un-serviceable. I was now the sole reconnaissance aircraft operating from Malta, in daylight, although the Group Captain did not inform me of that, at the time. He was inclined to regard the canopy as a trivial unnecessary adjunct without regard to the sortie I would be undertaking. This operation apparently meant flying at altitude – (25,000ft.) – for two or three hours, over the sea and enemy territory with the temperature outside at -20°C. Normally, with the canopy closed, the inside temperature at that height would be about up to +18°C which, while comfortable for the pilot, was primarily to keep the cameras operating. In consequence, there was no low temperature flying clothing available for me to use and the camera operation would be in jeopardy. The Group Captain had another idea. He suggested the canopy could be placed in position, closed, and the ground crews could somehow seal and fasten the canopy by 'tying it with string', with me inside. It was not put to me directly, as feasible, but I heard him suggest it to the ground crew as a solution to the problem. The idea of being sealed into the cockpit, with no escape until my return – in other words, being encapsulated – had no appeal whatsoever. All this debate took place beside the aircraft, between the Group Captain and the engineering staff. Whatever the solution, it appeared that I would have no say in it!

What was driving the Group Captain and his zeal for makeshift perhaps he knew himself, but I believed he was being chased by the AOC (Air Officer Commanding). The Engineering Officer and the NCO had declined to sign up the aircraft as serviceable: so, it all devolved on the new Pilot Officer, (me), to take the aircraft without it being signed up. Without a CO to act as intermediary for me, I was the 'fall guy'! Anyway, the canopy was fixed next day and I went off on a sortie in the usual way.

Again, to advance to a much later date and AB 300's major inspection – it was in fact, carried out in the open with the aircraft in pieces, propped up on lumps of Malta limestone. It looked terrible, until eventually, the inspection was declared complete. It was air-tested over the Island by various of us who by now comprised the flight, and for diverse 'snags', declared unserviceable again. Eventually, there were no more problems and it was put on the line for general day-to-day use. I do not seem to have had much trouble with it myself, as far as I remember, but I continued to receive complaints from the other pilots who often appeared to be glad to have made it back to the Island. I therefore approached the Engineering Officer to see if we could have it replaced. Receiving a negative reply, ostensibly because of lack of justification, I therefore took it upon my own Pilot Officer shoulders to say I would only authorise its use over Sicily and I was prepared to defend that decision. That was vindicated, finally, by its new engine failing over Sicily. The pilot survived, unhurt, but was taken as a prisoner-of-war. I had been flying it, AB 300, myself four days previously, on a shipping search to Messina, Palermo and Cape Bon when the enemy A/A had fired pointer rounds and I sighted 109s in pursuit of me.

In my early and solitary days, Laddie Lucas and Raoul Daddo-Langlois used to visit me from time-to-time, on bicycles. With most of their own aircraft unserviceable, they would make encouraging remarks about the work I was doing on my own. No one from 69 Squadron or the HQ ever acknowledged my solo act or indeed my existence. My first assistant to arrive was Sergeant Les R. Colquhoun, who walked in one day and introduced himself after I had been there a month or so. I explained the situation to him and we took it in turns from then on to photographically cover the operational orders as they appeared on the Form Greens, addressed to 69 Squadron and handed to me by the Luqa Intelligence Office. It appears a PRU OTU had been formed in UK and Colquhoun was a graduate and knew the form from practice. The next graduate to arrive was Flight Sergeant J.O. Dalley who similarly introduced himself and fell into line with the arrangements Colquhoun and I had made. Being first to arrive in the early morning, I, one day, found the AOC, Air Vice-Marshal H.P. Lloyd, unsmilingly inspecting my little office set-up. After exchanging time of day, to break the silence, I mentioned the good work Sgt. L.R. Colquhoun was doing and how he had settled down quickly into the routine. The AVM endorsed that with, what was news to me, that Colquhoun had achieved the first cover of some aspect or other in Sicily. As far as I knew, it was news to Colquhoun as well. We didn't receive comment, good or bad, about what we did as a rule. I was now operating with the help of three NCO pilots and we were kept very busy, which was a good thing. We all liked flying and there was nothing else to do, with Valetta in ruins. Food was short and the streets blocked with rubble. Bomb dodging was our chief 'recreation' when not flying. There was no social life.

The third NCO pilot to be 'shunted' into PR service at Luqa, was Frank Gillians from New Zealand. He unfortunately, was the pilot of AB 300 when its new engine failed over Sicily and he was impatient to tell me angrily about it when we both, as ex-prisoners of war, were repatriated to Britain in 1945. This situation arose in spite of the precautions I had taken to ensure, as far as I could, that a life was not lost unnecessarily by keeping AB 300 within the range of enemy or our own rescue services or a land mass, and at least I had achieved that.

Les Colquhoun was rewarded by the award of a DFM and this was followed by a Commission. The same for Jo Dalley – first a DFM then a Commission. Les C., on commissioning, joined me at Siggiewi, where we shared an acquisition of mine, the bicycle I had taken on charge, from a RAF friend who was gratefully leaving the Island on posting.

Day-to-day operations continued to be under my control although I had not been formally appointed Flight Commander. The 69 Squadron CO, Wing Commander Tennant, had disappeared one night, on what I understood was a familiarisation flight, which I did not find out about for some time. In any case, my only contact with him was when he signed my log book without my sighting him. This log book signature was our notification in the Flight that he had gone, when it changed to P/O Munro, 'Acting CO 69 Squadron'. The operation of the Marylands/Baltimores was quite a separate entity and although the Spitfires were attached to 69 Squadron there was little or no contact. We were, in the main, ignored by the 69 people. The bombing and strafing we were receiving precluded wandering about visiting other units, also there was an absence of invitations from anyone else. They knew where we were and we didn't know where they were. A few pilots from other units called in to greet us from time-to-time. Pilot Officer McKay, an Australian and Maryland/Baltimore pilot, was the main, and very welcome visitor in those hectic days. I believe he eventually became the CO of 69 Squadron as a Wing Commander.

My 'office' adjoined a long derelict room which, as buildings were steadily demolished by enemy action, became a crew assembly room for strike crews such as the torpedo carrying Beauforts. Numerous times I remember returning from a dawn reconnaissance to find Beaufort Squadron crews, mainly sitting on the floor, looking at me entering and for a sign from me that a convoy or Naval Unit had been found out there and, therefore, their destiny would be sealed – to go out and attack it. The high casualty rate of those Beaufort strikes made it an unenviable operation to be anticipating. I always felt sorry that my success in finding their targets had such unpleasant side effects for them even before the start of their mission.

Another arrival to swell the ranks of PRU, held the rank of flying officer and after he had become used to operating in the area, I gave him a trip to Benghazi, after briefing him on the requirement which was to ascertain if a certain tanker was in port there. On his return, when pressed, he said he was certain there was no tanker. Yes, he said he had taken photos but they would only show the same thing – no tanker. In consequence of the established reliability of our previous observations, a large strike planned for the tanker was stood down in the Middle East before the photographic interpreters declared that the tanker *was* in port. This was the first discordant note which, as a Flight, we had experienced and what is more, the same pilot resented being held responsible.

With the change in AOCs, from Air Vice-Marshal H.P.Lloyd to Air Vice-Marshal K. Park, our aircraft were summarily removed from the airfield to 'Safi' strip, a very rough area, along which, if you persevered, among the scrubby growth, bomb holes and wrecked aircraft, I believe you could reach Hal Far on the South of the Island. On asking, we were told, through third parties, it was because we were not fighters. We were using Mark IV PR Spitfires which were based on the Mark V fighter without armament. 'Only fighters were allowed to remain within the airfield perimeter.'

On the other hand, at almost the same time, Air HQ had also ordered PRU Spitfire early take-offs to be an hour before first light for convoy and similar Naval location and confirmation sorties. Because our aircraft had no cockpit night flying equipment this entailed us rigging up torches with rubber bands to odd fittings in the cockpit to cope with the night flying aspect of pre first light take-off and early course setting. It was also a good idea to take the torch for the last light sortie as well because of the possibility of being caught out by darkness. I wondered if there were any other RAF aircraft in service without cockpit lighting. This regime of an hour before first light take off combined with a midday sortie and a dusk landing were obviously, according to our thoughts on the subject, to keep tabs on the Italian Navy along with any Axis convoys in transit to North Africa.

It will be seen that any movement of the Italian Navy or Axis convoys would be readily apparent with a thrice daily check – beginning at dawn and ending at dusk. This coverage of the Axis craft was also ordered by AHQ whenever one of our own convoys was not only expected but also while they too were in transit. All this frenetic activity meant long hours in the air, all spent over the sea on one engine – fortunately, the reliable Rolls-Royce Merlin. In order to cover these thrice daily requirements for reconnaissance checks on the Italian fleet and convoys, with the aircraft and pilots available, I devised a flying programme of pilots on the before first light sorties, to do the dusk landing sortie, as well, on that day. Next day, those pilots would fly the midday sortie only then back to the early and late again, next day and so on. Five, six or seven hours flying in a day sometimes. Came August and we were busy with the above arrangement which worked well but kept every single one of us extended, flying every day, twice every other day, seven days a week.

Our unique flight, manned by genuinely skilful reconnaissance pilots like Les Colquhoun, Jo Dalley and Frank Gillions, worked very well without much supervision. We all complied with my programme and the air work called for by AHQ was completed on schedule.

Area covered operationally from Malta

CHAPTER FIVE

MALTA 1942 – A DAY IN THE LIFE

I find it impossible to remember every sortie which I completed during those hectic flying days in Malta. Therefore I have chosen one somewhat typical day in July which is an indication of the life we led.

The day I have chosen to feature is one where I would have been informed by the Form Green, (operations order), issued on the teleprinter by AHQ the day previously and consisting of what operations were expected to be performed by my Spitfire Flight. When issued this way I could make out a day's programme for my PRU which was composed of, at this time, myself, a pilot officer and three NCO pilots. The aircraft strength matched the pilots, i.e. four. My programme, which I posted on the board I had located at the table, required an individual pilot to carry out two sorties on one day and one the next. These schedules were my answer to the work load upon us with the four pilots and four aircraft.

In view of this arrangement, I had listed myself, as it was my turn, for a one hour before first light take-off next day, with a last light landing sortie as well. I walked home across the airfield and beyond to Siggiewi where I slept. After making a phone call to the 'Ops Room' to determine the 'state of the plot', i.e. whether any enemy or friendly aircraft were likely to be coming in, I would put a call into the guardroom for a 4 am wake-up call. I tended not to rely wholly on this and usually would waken myself. My sleeping quarters were a long way on foot and what with night bombing raids, the blackout and ill defined walking tracks, the calls sometimes failed to materialise in time.

On the way to bed, across the airfield, one would sometimes be confronted by an airman with a rifle who would demand, 'Halt, and come forward to be recognised with your hands up Sir!'.

Obviously I was a familiar figure. These incidents usually used to pass off quickly except for one night when the Station Commander, inexplicably, used his distinctive but on this night, somewhat slurred voice, to refer to me by name, to reinforce the sentry's order for me to drop my cycle which I was wheeling and to stand with my hands up above my head, in the torchlight. Perhaps he got a kick out of it but all I could think of was getting some sleep in anticipation of a long flying day beginning at four in the morning.

Having arrived at Siggiewi Signals Station, my bedroom was in a limestone block-built building with sparse but adequate furniture of bed and dresser. The former was equipped with a suspended mosquito net. There was usually bombing during the night and some bombs came close. One night a bomb seemed to have our name on it and in daylight it was revealed leaning against the stone fence outside the bedroom window. I heard it coming and thought, this is it, and when it arrived there was a tremendous thump and fortunately it did not go off.

In the small hours it was my lot, today, to be off across the dark airfield again with no sentries or tipsy Group Captains evident, to 'G' Shelter, where one of the controllers, such as Flight Lieutenant Dudley-Pope or Flight Lieutenant Gorst would receive my information about where I was headed in the Spitfire and my flight plan. In return, they would tell me what they knew of enemy activity and I would also contact the Met. Office for their estimates of what the wind and weather would do.

My parachute and helmet were in the miniature area I called an office – we all four kept our gear in a tall steel locker I had purloined. I kept my substitute authorisation book on the table where I would now make my entry and sign it. Then I would make my way to the aircraft, usually on foot, carrying my helmet and parachute, wearing my life-jacket and lighting my way by torchlight.

As I have already mentioned, after AVM Keith Park took over as AOC, we, in PRU, were banished off the airfield. All non-fighter aircraft had to go down to Safi Strip. The airfield at Luqa was to be inhabited only by fighter aircraft. So, one day, after the AOC's order had apparently been issued, I found all my aircraft had been moved to Safi. This was rather a 'jungle' strip of land running from Luqa all the way to Halfar – so it was said. I never got that far! On either side of it were bomb holes and some bomb craters on its rough surface. Among the holes and scrubby vegetation were bombed and burned out aircraft. There were other damaged aircraft on which repairs were being attempted – in all, general shambles prevailed. Now we were parked there. All the snags made taxying out of it in the dark, only possible with the energetic co-operation and athleticism of the ground crew, using a torch to indicate the safest route.

Our PR Mark IVs had no electric lights except the usual three coloured navigation lights; no landing or cockpit lights; no armament; normal Spitfire fuel capacity of approximately 90 gallons extended by two 66-gallon tanks being incorporated into the leading edge of both wings. Photographic equipment included two tandem-mounted cameras for vertical photography installed in the rear fuselage. Later models included an oblique camera.

The photographic equipment was all installed and serviced by the photographic tradesmen. Our job as pilots had developed into switching cameras on after placing the Spitfire accurately over the target straight and level. The control of the interval between exposures remained with the pilot and this in turn was influenced by wind and ground speed. Obviously, flying into wind the ground speed is reduced with a lengthened interval called for and vice versa.

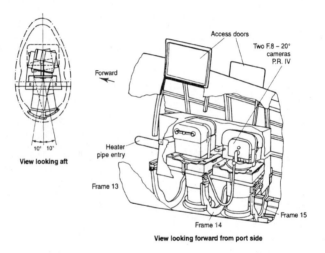

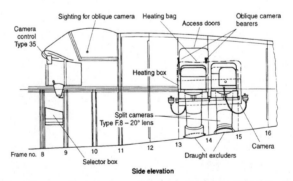

Tandem camera installation, Spitfire PR Mark IV

The installation of the tandem cameras towards the rear of the hatch on the port side, ensured the lenses were suspended over two optical flats situated in the bottom of the fuselage. The two cameras were installed so as to ensure their cover overlapped by 10 degrees laterally whilst the longitudinal cover lap remained under the control of the pilot. The pilot's ability or skill in judging the effect of wind on ground speed from high altitude over enemy territory was obviously brought into play in this aspect.

Two features concerning the cameras could completely spoil the effectiveness of an otherwise successful sortie. One was oil leaks from the engine which could flow back along the bottom of the fuselage and cover one or both of the optical flats, resulting in no pictures from the side(s) affected. The other fault being if the film was to break and therefore could not be transported on that camera. The pilot was usually unaware of these failures until a return to base was made and the camera serviced.

Some aircraft (persistent offenders), were fitted with a local modification in the form of a low V in plan form as a fairing ahead of the optical flat. This was an effort to hopefully divert an oil leak away from the optical flat and send it on down the fuselage.

Before starting up and taxying out of Safi, I had gone through the usual pre-flight inspection with my torch. The aircraft were always well presented by all the trades involved under very difficult circumstances. Our ground staff, two without exception, were on duty, in the dark, ready to see me off. Running-up had been banned by AHQ staff as well, to save fuel! At last, having gone through all the preliminaries, I had started up on the trolley accumulator and arrived at the airfield proper. The airman who had been running at the wing tip with his guiding torch, would jump up on the wing expecting and receiving his release. Before he left, he would point out any obstructions or delayed action bombs to be avoided. My guiding light then jumped down and vanished in the darkness. I moved the aircraft onto the runway with its shrouded lights and dark gaps and lined up. My radiator temperature, by this time, was high, but other indicators were normal. Synchronising the gyro direction indicator with the magnetic compass, I switched off the navigation lights, turned on the oxygen and made sure the torch in its rubber bands was secure and directed at the instrument panel. Down the runway and off into the blackness of the pre first-light sky.

This was a calm night similar to the one where I had been required by the Group Captain to drop my cycle, which I had been wheeling on the airfield and raise my hands above my head, creating an absurdity in the middle of these serious duties during the siege. Climbing today on 070°, our usual first course to the north, I reflected this morning that the Axis must have been getting their beauty sleep at this hour because I did not encounter any enemy opposition of any sort at this time, in the air or on the ground.

Sometimes in an unstable air mass the cumulo nimbus clouds could make things quite hectic. The Spitfire was a pleasant, sensitive, easy and gentle aeroplane to fly but on instruments, in turbulent cloud conditions, in the dark, with only a torch jiggling about for illumination, the situation could develop threateningly. One could blunder into cumulo nimbus in the dark quite easily but even the lightning reaching out from within one of these clouds as one flew past could be quite unsettling.

Continuing my climb, I reached and levelled off at the comfortable cruising altitude of twenty-five thousand feet over the sea on the way to the big Italian Naval base of Taranto, my main target. My engine was running well at what was now minus 2 lb boost pressure, giving me a calculated true air speed of just over three hundred miles per hour, which we were using in those days in keeping with the instrument calibration. Outside air temperature had dropped to minus 20°C whilst the aircraft heater kept the internal temperature at a pleasant, near plus 18°C. Hot air collected from behind the radiator and ducted into the fuselage provided this welcome facility – an essential for the cameras at these temperatures. The heater rarely failed but it was not unknown which then made the pilot regret his liquid intake before flight.

The sky in the east had become quite grey with the rapidly developing dawn, this giving me an horizon to fly by as I approached Taranto on a north-easterly course. The Italian gunners were soon awakened and my environment was becoming encumbered with flashes and residual puffs, as I made my first pass across the Harbour. Turning to make a photographic run I counted the battleships and noted the figure on my knee pad and then counted the cruisers. The battleships of the Italian Navy had distinctive diagonal red strips on the decks. These shapes were now visible and recognisable from practice. The flak had eased, then two near bursts again; I always felt these were indicators to their interceptor fighters. In the early morning light I had just discerned two monoplanes catching the sun, starting towards me from well below and, having completed my second run and count, I turned the cameras off and headed out to sea. I had a good start towards the south-east over the sea and forgot about my pursuers. Eventually when well away from the coast I curved away south and then headed south-west. I didn't see my pursuers again.

On this particular sortie, my detail was to fly back to Malta as quickly as possible to report the remaining Naval strengths. It was too early for good photographic light but it was considered advisable to turn the cameras on just in case, as confirmation. Sometimes, a self-evident code report of the situation was required by radio but not this time. The sun was up now and distant Mount Etna, with its plume, looked a wonderful sight, lighted from the east as did the white houses dotting the mountainous state of Calabria. Those white buildings catching the low rising sun from the east always looked to me like pebbles on a beach as I headed back south to 'home' base and breakfast which would include one of my four half slices of daily bread but that was to come. At the moment, out over the sea, I could enjoy the view. These early morning vistas in the Mediterranean never failed to impress me with their breath-taking beauty. About a hundred miles away from base I lowered the nose and began reducing height whilst increasing my speed which I believe gave the plotting people, back at Malta, a busier time moving their frames on the plotting table as a result of the radar operators picking me up. A very fast low pass over the Intelligence office announced my return.

After landing at Luqa, the ground crew wanted to know about any aircraft 'snags' which required rectification; then as I climbed out, the photographic man presented his form which I filled in on the wing tip as he removed the magazine from the tops of the two cameras. The details required were obviously places photographed, height, number of exposures, time etc. Really, in reply, my only complaint or 'snag' to report was that I had belatedly discovered as I joined the airfield circuit on return, that the radio was not working and it transpired that in consequence I had returned and landed while a raid alert was in progress. It seems power packs oiling up were often the cause of these Radio Telephone failures.

After the photographer and radio man and the rigger and fitter had questioned me, I was on my way to the Intelligence Section while the photographer took the camera magazines by motor transport to the AHQ in Valetta. On my way, carrying my flying gear and parachute, I was amused to see one of our ground crew streaking across the aircraft area and I knew where he was going. He would be making for the Martello tower which stood near or on the airfield boundary with Luqa village. This lad had salvaged a couple of working Browning machine-guns from one of the many aircraft wrecks strewn about. He had contrived to mount one of these guns on the turret top of the ancient tower and whenever a raid approached and usually when the Klaxon had sounded, he would rush over and man his gun to shoot at anything which came close enough to be within firing range. One day when we were watching, a Ju 87, (Stuka), had obviously seen what was happening and it dive-bombed the tower.

We saw this incident and the Stuka pilot's aim was accurate. We saw the bomb leave the aircraft and curve down to land at the foot of the Martello. It did not explode! The occupant gunner was peering down with his hands on the parapet where the bomb had penetrated at the base of the structure. He resembled one of those wartime drawings, 'Kilroy was here'. We thought we had lost him that time but no, there he was, at it today as enthusiastically as ever with his special anti-aircraft position. Incidentally, he claimed to have found his mark on an enemy aircraft but not that one.

On this occasion, having observed the Martello gunner on his way to 'his' tower, I continued my pedestrian way with an eye on the sky because experience had demonstrated the ability of the 109s to sneak in unannounced, as it were. One such incident I had observed, occurred after the alert had sounded when a stranger aircraft in the form of a Bristol Beaufort torpedo-bomber landed and at the end of his landing run turned cross wind and stopped. Two 109s appeared, as if from nowhere and flew along the runway at nought feet, firing at the stationary Beaufort. Not content with one pass they pulled up and made around for another go, to finish off the job. This time, however, the Bofors AA gunners' aim was good and the No. 2 109 lost his tail. The No. 1 flew flew off home to Sicily alone. There were horrific injuries in the Beaufort torpedo bomber, of personnel and aircraft. That was that occasion. I continued my perambulation to the Intelligence Office where I put my parachute and helmet on the floor and the chief, Flight Lieutenant Kerridge, interrogated me on where, how, how much etc. Enemy action observed and or suffered, photographic runs and height along with any other relevant details on my sortie. The IO then obtained the Met. Officer, Mr Davis on the line and handed me over to him for a further questionnaire.

During this interrogation time, the air raid must have been developing because the Bofors gun emplacement Klaxon sounded its strident warning and we all, those in the Intelligence Office, made our way smartly to the cover of the local surface shelter or down the steps to the below-ground one dug into the limestone at the end of the building. Most of us made for the close-by surface shelter which was covered with an anti-shrapnel roof layer of earth and rock from where it was possible to sneak a look at the approach

Seen at Wigram in New Zealand back in 1934, this Bristol Fighter had seen service in India since the end of the Great War, but had been replaced by Wapitis and Harts.

An unusual visitor to Wigram, this Seagull amphibian was spotted in 1934.

This is a general view of the CAC fleet at Wigram in 1938. The RNZAF control tower and admin. buildings are under construction.

This Zögling primary glider was the sole equipment of the Canterbury Glider Club. The design originated in Germany in the early 1920s and was copied widely throughout the world during later years.

The author, right, with the Miles Hawk of the Canterbury Aero Club at Wigram in 1938.

DH60 Gipsy Moth ZK-AGU of the Canterbury Aero Club. It was built by de Havilland students at Hatfield in the UK and was the aircraft in which I first went solo in 1939.

Canterbury Aero Club pilots and instructors pose in front of the club's Monospar aircraft at Wigram just before the outbreak of war in 1939. The author is standing in the back row, in front of the aircraft's nose.

At elementary flying training school, Harewood, New Zealand, in 1941. The author is on the right, standing in front of a line-up of de Havilland Tiger Moths.

The author in 1941.

Members of 10 Course at RNZAF Harewood in 1941 before departing for Canada. The aircraft is a Blackburn Baffin.

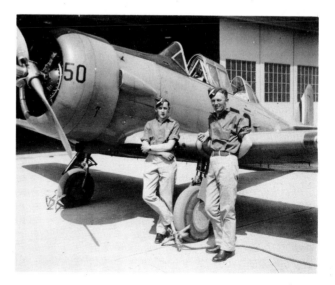

May 1941 at the RAF Flying Training School at Moose Jaw in Canada in front of one of the Harvards.

No 66 Squadron at RAF Perranporth in October 1941.
Back row left to right: Flying Officer Bruce Tidy (Engineering Officer), Pilot Officer Mann (Adjutant), Pilot Officer Gatty May (Pilot) RAAF, Pilot Officer Raoul Daddo Longlois (Pilot) RAF, Pilot Officer Matheson (Pilot) RNZAF, Pilot Officer Coldbeck (Pilot) RNZAF, an Irish pilot, Pilot Officer 'Laddie' Lucas (Pilot) RAF.
Front row left to right: Flying Officer (Intelligence Officer) RAF, Flight Lieutenant ('B' Flight Commander) RAF, Squadron Leader 'Dizzie' Allen DFC (OC 66 Squadron) RAF, Capitaine Claisse (Pilot) Free French, Medical Officer.

RAF Perranporth, 1941.
Left to right:
Flight Sergeant Robinson
(Senior NCO Fitter), Sergeant
Pilot Laurie Verrall RNZAF and
Pilot Officer Coldbeck.

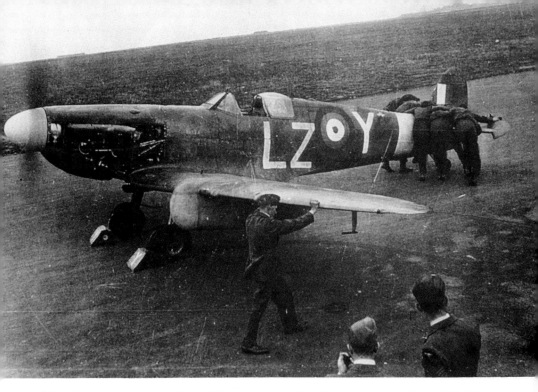

A Spitfire IIA running-up with five holding down the tail, taken at Perranporth in 1941. This was the version of the Spitfire flown by 66 Squadron when the author joined it in 1941. This rare photograph shows the ugly 30 gallon fuel tank permanently fixed to the port wing. On take-off with the tank full, it was essential to open up very slowly and keep everything in the top-right-hand corner until there was sufficient slip-stream over the empennage to maintain directional control. The alternative, which was often practised by enthusiastic newcomers on a scramble take-off (and even seasoned pilots), was an uncontrolled swing off the runway. (P.B. Lucas)

'Laddie' Lucas (left) with the CO of 66 Squadron at that time, Squadron Leader Athol Forbes DFC, who is wearing the Polish Virtuli Militari which the Poles awarded to him for leading a flight in 303 Squadron in the 'Battle of Britain'. The late Athol Forbes became an Air Commodore before retirement.

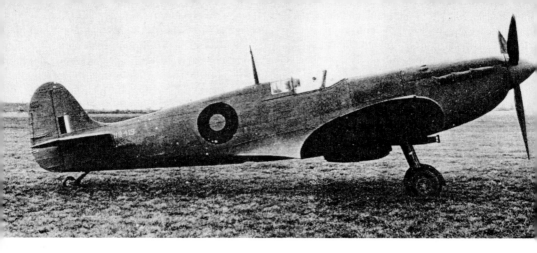

A Spitfire PR IV. These aircraft were converted from Spitfire Mk Vs and were often referred to in service as Mk VDs. The PR IV should not be confused with the experimental Spitfire Mk IV, powered by the Griffon engine.

A model of the author's Spitfire PR IV that was shot down on 10 November 1942. It is in the museum at Augusta in Sicily in the care of Dr Tullio Marcon.

of the formations or single enemy aircraft and further assess our chances. Some of the late assessments suggested it might have been wiser to go below into the rock shelter! In consequence there were sometimes some hurried last minute adjustments to that effect. It was usually possible to locate the approaching enemy by the bursts of heavy ack ack in the sky. Sometimes, the formations would appear to be heading straight for us then curve away to the Grand Harbour area where we could easily identify which bombs had fallen in the water by the shaking which accompanied the blast. At other times the Ju 88s and Stukas would make straight for us on the airfield when a further selection of aircraft and buildings would probably be made unusable and numerous holes in the airfield/runway surface would have to be filled in before flying could take place again. The heavy mechanised roller was a very precious piece of equipment at this time, having its own special shelter to which it was hurriedly retired before any raid developed. Because of hundreds of continuous raids by enemy aircraft, both by bombers and fighters, our buildings continued to disappear along with serviceable aircraft.

The raid, apparently over, although the 'All Clear' had not been sounded, we all returned to what we were doing before the Klaxon sounded. The Klaxon would sound again if further action threatened. Having finished the questionnaire, I would put my parachute, life jacket and helmet away and go to breakfast which was usually the monotonous thin slice of Bully beef and as I was thinking about when I approached the Island earlier, one of my four half slices of bread which was entered against my name in a ledger. A cup of weak urn tea with Carnation milk from a rusty tin which had been salvaged from the bombed freighter *Breckonshire* while lying on its side in Kalafrana Bay, completed that slimming diet breakfast. The *Breckonshire* had survived numerous attacks both en route to Alexandria, returning there empty and also heading to Malta again with now most urgently required supplies of every description. An intensive attack as she was being towed after bomb damage on her last voyage, made it imperative that she reach the 'sanctuary' of Kalafrana Bay. Unfortunately, however, there in the Bay the aerial attacks continued ferociously, until the vessel lay on her side. This was the top side protruding from the water where a hole had been made through which, in lulls in the attacks, anything which could be reached, was salvaged such as the rusting tins of Carnation milk I have just mentioned.

Once raids such as we had witnessed at Luqa and accompanying fighters had cleared, one could reasonably go about the further duties of the day. Being mid-summer, sitting at the table in my micro office checking on the progress of my flying programme, hearing from the other pilots and the NCO i/c servicing, I began to feel the heat as the temperature climbed and the effect of my early morning flight to Taranto and back. Being the only officer in my little unit at this time, the Intelligence Office used to load me with mail censoring whenever they could. I did some of these then there was my preparation for the last-light landing sortie of my own. In this latter connection, the IO called me to the telephone where a caller from AHQ. Air Staff was requesting an especially watchful eye to be kept on the 'E' Boats by shadowing them at Lampedusa, an Italian island about a hundred miles West of Malta, which was towards the Tunisian Coast. The 'E' boats were a very active part of the German and Italian Maritime armoury and usually seemed to be based in the Agrigento Harbour on the South Coast of Sicily but on this occasion, Lampedusa, a long flat island, seemed to be the basis for their activity. My orders now, were to shadow until dusk, in time for a last-light landing, back on Malta.

While in the vicinity of Lampedusa, there was heavy AA fire each time I approached the island but fortunately, no damage was done to my aircraft so I continued with my surveillance. I had calculated my arrival back at Malta to be at dusk and as it happened, my arrival coincided with the tail end of an Axis bombing raid with a lot of fighter activity both Axis and our own. My approach to Luqa was signalled by red tracer coming up and fortunately past me in the failing light. I had checked my IFF, (Identification, friend or foe), was switched on, so my only recourse was to call up fighter control on the VHF and tell them I was being fired on by our own guns and request them to inform the gunners.* This was immediately followed by a fighter Spitfire making a pass at me – obviously taking his cue from the Bofors firing at me. I turned into him, with more tracer passing me from behind until I spoke to him on the VHF channel which fortunately he was apparently tuned to and using.

After this encounter, I landed and handed my aircraft over to the groundcrew and made my report to Intelligence and the Met. Office. By then it was nightfall and I had what passed for an evening meal. After conferring with Operations regarding the state of the plot, I made my way across the airfield to Siggiewi and sleep. Tomorrow

---

* The Army Gunnery Officer, in charge of the Bofors gun firing at me, came to the Mess afterwards and declared to me he was just about to switch his gun to automatic before my complaint on the radio. 'We'd have got you if we'd done that!' he said matter of factly. I didn't hear from the Spitfire pilot.

promised to be a relative holiday as I had programmed myself, since it was my turn, to do the midday sortie. There would be no 3 or 4 am beginning and ending in the dark, for one day anyhow. Just a midday trip right across the Mediterranean to Navarino of about 800 miles, a round trip across the sea to the southern tip of Greece.

CHAPTER SIX

LUQA OPERATIONS

From 7 March 1942 when I first flew AB 300 into Malta, from UK, my airborne activity was initially concentrated on teaching myself the technique of operationally photographing the Sicilian airfields with their heavy populations of fighters and bombers. The harbours, too, provided plenty of fascination and scope with their remarkable numbers of flying boats, floatplanes and of course the Italian Navy. As stated previously, after a month I was joined by Sergeant L.R. Colquhoun.

For one short time our daily surveys of Axis airfields in Sicily, included line overlaps by Les Colquhoun and myself of large areas of the Catania Plains. This was brought about after the sharp eyes of the photographic interpreters Flt Lt Howard Colvin and Flt Lt Raymond Herschel, spotted a ground strip being prepared on the plains which had all the potential of a glider take-off area. The area photographed was accidentally covered by one of us on photo overun from Gerbini airfield and gave further grounds to the rumours of an invasion of Malta, which it was alleged, was being prepared by the Axis powers, to be launched against us from Sicily. The imperturbable Les Colquhoun and I had a rather uncomfortable session each on different days, stooging up and down straight and level on parallel tracks. I was expecting at anytime to be overwhelmed by Messerschmitt 109s or Machi 202s until we had covered most of the possible areas being prepared for glider launchings. In the event, nothing untoward happened, even though we could easily see the airfields of Gerbini and Catania with their touchy defences.

Our operation uncovered many more strips which didn't go any way towards calming the official attitude and their apprehensions. In time the panic subsided and we have since learned that Hitler himself cancelled the invasion of Malta, for which the strips were in fact a preparation. That cancellation of the invasion is now classed as one of Hitler's big mistakes and an opportunity missed as Malta was in a terribly weakened state. Nevertheless, Malta was revived and became a determining factor in the desert war by limiting supplies to Rommel.

Another month and Flight Sergeant J.O. Dalley walked in and he joined Les Colquhoun and myself with our continued surveillances. June 1942 saw the arrival of a fourth member, Sergeant Frank Gillions. The same month also saw something of a change in, or extension of, our targets from Sicily and related mainland and islands to more overseas – in relation to Malta – areas. Tripoli had been briefly ordered in March, however, June saw us visiting the island of Sardinia in the north-west and the large Taranto Naval Base in the north-east.

July brought the first of our visits to North Africa proper, in the form of Photo Reconnaissances to Benghasi with, of course, as usual quite a number of trips to Naples, Sardinia and all the islands such as Lampedusa, Pantellaria and the Tunisian coast and on to Tunis and Bizerta. As the month wore on, after an initial shock, we became used to Form Green orders including targets on the Greek west coast. We now became quite familiar, after the sea crossing, with the sight of the islands Zante, Cephalonia and Corfu, further north. Navarino harbour on the southern tip of the Greek west coast and in the middle, Patras, had their share of our attention too.

September regrettably brought our first casualty. As mentioned earlier, Frank Gillions failed to return with AB 300. By this time we had been joined by two more pilots. One being Adrian Warburton, DSO, DFC, who was promoted to Squadron Leader a day or so after his arrival and apparently appointed CO of 69 Squadron. There was no notice to me or introduction of any sort.

Meanwhile, before this happened, we had become familiar with all manner of nautical targets such as convoys, harbours and naval vessels at sea and in port, as well as continuing to photograph the tremendous array of aircraft on the Axis airfields. Daily ranging far and wide on what now amounted to a five hundred mile radius of Malta, I suppose we could have been termed 'The Unarmed Rovers' if anyone had thought of it.

There was no preamble to this change or extension of our duties to General Reconnaissance. I suppose we in Photographic Reconnaissance, being attached to 69 Squadron, the AHQ Malta thought that addressing our tasks to that Squadron, with their establishment of reconnaissance pilots and navigators, we would have their backing. However, the scene was originally set for us when the 69 Squadron CO, Wing Commander Tennant said to me 'I don't know anything about PRU, you'll have to look after yourself.' – and that, from the inception, is what I/we did. Pilot Officer McKay was one of our few contacts and that on a casual basis, within 69 Squadron.

Some of the targets which appeared summarily on Form Greens alongside our daily dicing targets in Sicily etc., we had never heard of previously and it was necessary to scramble for a map, find out where they were and how to get there. Some places, like Navarino, meant flying 400 hundred miles across the open Mediterranean and the same back again: back again often to find the small island of Malta under attack. If we were to miss the island by not too wide of the mark and it was light enough, we could go on up to Sicily to pin-point ourselves. Whilst we did carry a VHF set in our Spitfires, as mentioned, there was a tendency for the radio to fail because, we were told, the power packs oiled up on the long flights. In response to a technical NCO's suggestion we tried switching the radio off when away from the island, but this had only marginal success with frustration in bad weather or poor light conditions when we tried to restart it. Also, when listening out, we could judge how the battle was going and how best to handle our returning approach. Without radio, as has been mentioned, one could barge on into a dog fight or other enemy/friendly activity.

It was sometimes to be wondered who, on the Air Staff, was deciding these targets and times for our services. We had never had a visit from anyone except that early one I have mentioned by the AOC himself. At that time, Les Colquhoun and I were new and our activities were mainly applied to Sicily. For instance, one late afternoon, the local IO told me they had a request from AHQ for a 69 Squadron aircraft to make a photo reconnaissance of Suda Bay in Crete. We had never been given Suda Bay as a target previously. A quick reference to a map to measure the course and distance confirmed it was on the very edge of our range which also meant that it would be dark before a return could be made. My reply to Intelligence was, therefore, that it was too late for our aircraft as they were not equipped for night flying. An hour before first light in the morning would be appropriate. What I had in mind also was the difficulty, even impossibility, of finding a blacked out Malta after dark without aircraft lights or any aids for the solo pilot. This was the first new assignment beyond our present capability.

On the bomb and splinter-ravaged Luqa airfield itself, the building where the Intelligence Office was situated, was the same one in which my self-constructed PRU, 'office' existed. The salvaged furniture created a miniature haven in which to retreat and meet the other two,

Les Colquhoun and Jo Dalley, later also, Frank Gillions, at the end of a reconnaissance sortie or Axis raid. Also in this building was a longish unfurnished bomb-damaged room where, at this hectic time of the summer siege of 1942, the Beaufort strike crews gathered awaiting instructions. It was here too, as they waited for our return from a sortie, that we came face to face with them and their realisation of the casualties they faced as a result of our reports of maritime sightings. The Beaufort torpedo-bombers had an unenviable reputation and their task of approaching enemy shipping at low level to drop their torpedoes made them extremely vulnerable and, of course, the crews knew it. In this building also was situated a solitary manual telephone and from time-to-time I would be called by one of the Intelligence staff to take a call in their office. Usually it was the Senior Air Staff Officer (SASO), Group Captains Bowen-Buscarlet and Riley, are names that come to mind of that time. Conversations, on occasion, went like this. 'Coldbeck, I want you to fly out to the Greek Coast.' – which was about 400 miles to the east – 'to the vicinity of the island of Zante.' – (or some other geographical point he would name), 'then proceed south.' (or north, as the case may be and which he would detail). He would then probably cover his verbal instructions with a teleprinter at a later time. 'See what you can find of interest to us – do what you can, old chap.' On some occasions this would be varied by the SASO saying, 'As soon as you have a sighting and you come within R/T range, give us a call, "the oranges are red."' A call like this would indicate I had sighted a quarry. A strike force, standing by, could then be alerted immediately.

There were a variety of times for these reconnaissance operations to start and the orders were arriving at all times of the day, as distinct from our regular surveillance of the enemy ports and airfields which could be usually programmed the day previously. The hour before first-light take-off would get us to the Greek coast by dawn when the sun was coming over the horizon and in the clear weather which often prevailed in summer in the Middle Mediterranean, an arrow-head formation formed by a ship's wake was clearly visible to us at considerable distance from the height of 25,000 feet. That height was our favourite cruising altitude, in the Spitfire PR Mark IV, the aircraft we were using.

After pre-first-light take-off on these sorties to the Eastern Mediterranean our heading to the Greek coast would give us the earliest horizon to fly by. It will be appreciated however that flying to the east before dawn without cockpit lighting left the cockpit and dials in darkness until the sun came over the horizon. Flying across

71

the wide open spaces of the Mediterranean, especially in the first light hours of the day, didn't allow any map reading so it was just a matter of sitting there on the hard folded rubber dinghy, on top of the parachute, whilst steering accurately the course each of us had worked out for ourselves, using the Met. wind which the forecaster had 'prescribed' for 25,000 feet, or such other height which we had requested and the weather might dictate.

Approaching the estimated time of arrival (ETA) for the Greek coast, we would have to peer ahead into the lightening sky to try to make out where the landfall would be. If there were some fractured clouds about it was, at times, difficult to tell the islands or coastline from the shadows, but that situation would be improving all the time with increasing light and the reducing distances. The Rolls-Royce Merlin engine would meanwhile be working away in the front, like the faithful friend it was to those of us who had to fly over this bright blue sea every day and had, perforce, to trust it implicitly.

About this time in the flight it would be possible to finally switch off the torch in the rubber band 'mounting'. A typical landfall would be the Greek island of Zante; a shallow turn south would enable the search to be made, looking over the starboard wing along the increasingly sunlit sea, in the hope of seeing the telltale arrowhead pattern on the surface which we had come to expect a convoy in motion to make. Without that pattern to guide the eye, stationary vessels were very difficult, if not impossible, to spot from 25,000 feet in this early light.

Proceeding parallel to the distant coast and along the north/south axis of Zante, a thorough search of the glistening sea surface could be made, looking as far as possible under any broken cloud, for signs of a quarry. Quite often this arrowhead pattern would be partly obscured by these broken clouds so that two converging lines might be spotted between two clouds. By following the direction of convergence, with luck the tip of the arrow might be found in the open, beyond the cloud cover. Embedded within the arrowhead would be the plan shapes of the vessels and as time had passed in this job, those of us now comprising the flight had learned to recognise, with the help of the photographic interpreters, Colvin and Herschel, what these plan shapes meant: merchant vessels and their tonnage; naval cruisers; destroyers; E-boats, etc. We could tell what vessels we were looking down on, as a whole convoy and escort ploughed its way towards the south where the Axis forces on the African continent waited for their supplies of fuel, ammunition, rations and transport. For example, on one such morning, a convoy sighted was recognised as consisting of a tanker with an escort of four destroyers. Once a convoy had been sighted, its position, composition, heading and estimated speed would be noted as accurately as possible on the knee pad. Photographic confirmation would be sought by flying along the directional axis of the convoy, using the split vertical cameras mounted behind the pilot. At that time of day it was fairly poor light down there on the surface of the sea but there was nothing to lose by exposing a few feet of film and if there were some images, however poor, there was always the possibility that the photographic interpreters would be able to make something of them. (A follow-up sortie in full daylight could be mounted if necessary to make a positive identification).

Notes having been made and photographs taken, a turn away could be made towards the west and the home base of Luqa. About two hundred miles into the return leg to base, it was usually possible to call up to test reception and get a faint reply. Having passed the message in self-evident code language, as had been instructed by the SASO, Base usually appeared to have no difficulty in accepting the message, although they could hardly be heard on the aircraft radio. No doubt the operators would have been briefed to expect a call from a returning Spitfire. It was quite often a lovely morning over the Mediterranean with the light now behind the aircraft as it headed for Malta and with the snow-covered summit of Mount Etna just appearing low down on the horizon far away to the right and illuminated by the rising sun. This was a bonus. It was so peaceful – no Ju 88s or Stukas diving and bombs falling or guns banging away. It seemed as if it was almost unreal, in the light of what was happening on the island and elsewhere. Paradisical, if there is such a word. It made one wish it could go on forever. The memory of those lovely mornings and seascapes are with me today. Further into the homeward journey the chief controller's voice, Group Captain Woodhall, at times addressed the returning pilot to say there were some 'big jobs' (bombers) present at base together with escorting 'small jobs'. 'Keep a good lookout', he would say, 'you may have to stand off.' Obviously, on most occasions, fighter control would be keeping an eye on our expected approaches by radar but there was the odd time when we would be temporarily regarded as an enemy and an interception attempted by the Malta fighters. If ordered to 'stand off', it was usual to make for the south of the island to wait there until entry became a little less congested as sometimes happened with large numbers of Axis bombers, with fighters, and our own fighters, mixing it over the island.

We, in the PRU at Luqa, Les Colquhoun, Jo Dalley and myself, had come to expect that our forces in the Mediterranean, consisting of aircraft, naval surface craft and submarines would ultimately be sent to attack what we reported. But we were all puzzled by directives from the Air Staff about where we were guided to seek the enemy. Later, there were others – Frank Gillions, and even, eventually, in mid-August, Warburton. We were to go out and find convoys and all sorts of individual and groups of naval units. Almost invariably these turned up where we sought them. Such wonderful intelligence was remarkable and we often wondered how our seniors on the Air Staff obtained such information. Another factor in the mystery was the plain language, self-evident messages which we were, from time to time, instructed to transmit to base.

It was in 1974 that a book was launched, entitled *The Ultra Secret* by E.W. Winterbotham, Chief of the Air Department of the Secret Intelligence, (MI6), 1930–1945. In his book he revealed how, early in the War, capturing the German Enigma machine (Ultra) messages were intercepted and the exact placement of forces, units and ships became known. It was imperative that the knowledge thus obtained be kept secret so that the enemy was unaware of the Allied knowledge. We can see now, that although, in the case of my PRU flight, we were going out to find enemy units, ships etc., which were possibly known about already, and we were the means of justifying that knowledge. It wouldn't take the enemy listening service very long to work out where we had been or that we had found a quarry.

With the recent publication of the latest of Roy C. Nesbit's splendid books, *The Armed Rovers*, I noticed a picture of an Axis ship on fire. This was a photograph I took on 17 August that year, 1942. This was the second time I photographed that convoy on 17 August. This picture appeared in an HMSO publication *The Air Battle of Malta* published in 1944 and a copy of which has recently been generously supplied to me by Jim Allen, of Surrey who in those days was a very active Radio Telephonist in Malta fighter control. The photographic section thought enough of the ship photo to supply me with a personal copy in 1942 but it disappeared from my effects after that 10 November 'incident' of mine which is narrated in detail appropriately later in this story.

On 17 August I was on a sortie to Trapani in the west of Sicily in Spitfire BR 665, then across the base of the Tyrrhenian Sea section of the Mediterranean to Sardinia. Having completed my Photographic Reconnaissance there of Cagliari, Elmas, Deccimomanu and San Pietro Island on the south-west corner of Sardinia, I set off for Malta again on the direct route through the Sicilian Straits area.

Approaching the island of Pantellaria, I sighted a merchant vessel which I estimated to be about 7000 tons, accompanied in convoy by two destroyers; 320° Pantellaria 4 miles. Having photographed the convoy I resumed my homeward course. Flying time on landing was four hours ten minutes. That same day I was in the same aircraft, refuelled and camera magazines changed, on my way back to find the convoy again, or what was left of it, the Beaufort torpedo-bombers having attacked it after I was there earlier that day. I photographed the now stationary smoking vessel which I recorded was down by the bow and I noted one of the destroyers leaving for the north, (Sicily).

The whole area of the operation had moved south and east to the vicinity of Lampedusa, 290° 45 miles. There were now several enemy aircraft present and I noted six fighters and four Ju 88s.

There was an element of mystery about the enemy aircraft which had now appeared and were flying around the ship and the retreating destroyer. They didn't seem interested in chasing me who was above them and could view them easily. Perhaps they had been sent on anti-submarine duties and didn't really expect a Spitfire out there in the wide open ocean so far from Malta, (150 miles). If they were looking for signs of a submarine they would be looking down and missed me lurking above them. The anti-submarine idea occurred to me because while circling the ship and its fighters and Ju 88s, there were numerous volcanoes of water arising in the vicinity which I could only assume had been initiated by the attendant destroyer. Depth charges?

Completing my photography for the second time, I moved off back to Malta. Flying time from take-off to landing – two hours. Roy C. Nesbit records that the vessel which he names as *Rosalino Pilo* was finally sunk that evening by the submarine HMS *United*.

CHAPTER SEVEN

LAST DAYS in MALTA

A day or so prior to 10 August 1942, I received a note from AHQ addressed to me personally and accompanying a medium sized packet which in turn was addressed, of all places, to the Regia Aeronautica in Sicily. The note requested me to 'drop the package at Catania, without endangering the aircraft, next time I was up that way'. Just like that! No other explanation or directions of timing or height. Catania was an almost daily target of our PRU flight because it always contained a great many aircraft as did its neighbour, Gerbini, a little further west. The thing about Catania and Gerbini was that we all knew we would be sure of heavy flak there, especially at any height below 25,000 feet. Now, I thought to myself, a simple brown paper package dropped from an aircraft travelling at 300 mph at that sort of altitude (of 25,000 ft.), would land anywhere or nowhere, i.e. never be found.

I had discovered from the Intelligence section, that this packet contained letters and other keepsakes of the Italian crew of the Cant float-plane which the South African Air Force officer, Lt Strever and his crew, comprising an English RAF Officer and two Royal New Zealand Air Force NCOs had captured while they were being transferred as prisoners-of-war from the vicinity of the island of Corfu to the Italian mainland at Taranto. Strever and his Beaufort crew had been shot down whilst attacking a ship which, in the dawn, I had located off the Greek coast after a pre first-light take-off, on the day on which they were later sent out to attack it.

The crew had been rescued by an Italian Cant float-plane and had been taken as prisoners of war to its base at Prevesa where they were extremely well treated – given good meals and their clothes dried with comfortable beds to sleep in and in some cases vacated by their captors to accommodate them. It was next day, in the course of being transferred to the Italian mainland at Taranto, on the way into captivity, that the Allied Beaufort crew saw an opportunity to take over the Cant float-plane on which they were travelling. They hated having to do this to their hospitable enemy and it appears it was in appreciation of the kindness shown to them by the Italians, that I was being asked to make this drop of these letters and personal items, at the heavily defended enemy base of Catania on the east coast of Sicily.

In an effort to ensure it was not a wasted gesture, I obtained some long lengths of serrated edged fabric used on fabric-covered aircraft – e.g. Swordfish – and I spent some time on the floor copying the address from the package, in red chalk, along each streamer which I tied securely to the package.

My next flight north was to photograph Naples Harbour, passing clear of Catania where I decided I would make the drop on the way home through Messina on the north-east corner of Sicily. I photographed an Axis convoy of one merchant vessel escorted by a destroyer, on the way. Southbound after Messina I began reducing my height from 25,000 feet, my cruising altitude, because I had decided I had to be quite low, for the drop to be effective. I had rolled the serrated edged tape around the package to which it was attached and tucked the whole between my thigh and parachute because there was nowhere else for it to go. As I approached the airfield, south of Mount Etna, I slowed right down and opened the hood. Putting the Spitfire into a steep turn over the airfield at about 3,000 feet, I threw the parcel down and out with the end of the tape through my fingers so that the streamers would stream out and so be conspicuous as the package fell. To my surprise all remained quiet as far as I was aware. I then made my exit out to the east coast again as fast as possible. I often wondered about the real success of this little operation. I had to wait 52 years for the answer.

It was only comparatively recently, in 1994, that I saw a letter in the Aircrew Association magazine, *Intercom* written by an Englishman, Dennis Maccagno, who is of Italian extraction. His cousin, who lives in Turin, was on that Cant Squadron at the time and they wondered what had become of their Squadron float-plane which, of course, the letters I had dropped, explained. Dennis had been in touch with his cousin who revealed that the crew, whose mail I dropped, had become PoWs and in due course, some of them went to Canada until they were repatriated at the European war's end in May 1945. The cousin also wrote to me giving positive confirmation that the Catania mail drop was collected in good condition and forwarded on to the relatives and next of kin etc. He also told me that those of his Squadron who surrendered to the RAF when Italy capitulated, were kept on flying for the Allies while, sadly, of those who surrendered to the

Axis powers, some, I believe, fared badly and others sent to work in concentration camps in Germany.

We now return to August 1942, on Malta. This was the time of the assembly and arrival of what remained of the largest convoy, Pedestal, to set course for Malta from Gibraltar. This August convoy when I first saw it, off Bizerta, had already been badly mauled and the story of it has been well covered in many volumes elsewhere. It was a remarkable sight from my aircraft and as the ships progressed towards the east, a pilot could navigate simply by following the oil slicks as well as by the burning and abandoned wrecks, all the way to Malta. Two of these vessels were conspicuous – the *Ohio* and the *Brisbane Star* with all manner of terrible things happening to others I could not identify but which I photographed for reference at AHQ.

It was after I had been on one of these sorties over the sea far away from Malta that I was alone sitting on my office seat reflecting and attending to censoring letters and the programme for the morrow when I was surprised by a Flight Lieutenant walking in silently behind me in desert boots. I recognised him as the person I had seen 'holding court' in the bar at Luqa, in March, at the time I had first transferred myself and AB 300 from Takali. Yes, it must be Flight Lieutenant Warburton. I said, 'Just in?' He answered 'Yes'. then he quickly reversed and disappeared. As on the first occasion, no names were exchanged. It was several days later that he appeared again – now wearing the rank badges of Squadron Leader. Jo Dalley, who always seemed to be first with the news on the bush telegraph, told me that Adrian Warburton was now CO of 69, re-named Reconnaissance Squadron, to be composed of three flights, one of the Marylands/Baltimores, another, the ASV Wellingtons and one of the PRU Spitfires. I had no similar indication from Warburton, or anyone else but the idea gained credence. I asked the new Squadron Leader, when I had the chance, if he would be flying with us and received an affirmative. I put him on the programme after enquiring if the sortie I offered would be convenient to him. That worked for a short time but very soon he began to ignore my programme and without reference to me he would take a Spitfire and head off in it. This played havoc with our schedule, trying to keep up with the requirements of AHQ with the very limited aircraft available. A pilot on my programme would go out to the dispersal and find his sortie and aircraft had disappeared. The ground crew would confirm that Squadron Leader Warburton was flying it although the Form 700 would not have been signed. On his return, the Squadron Leader would take a seat in the Intelligence Office to reveal then where he had been and the tremendous adventures he had endured to get his photographs. His voice travelled through the building which provoked some of my pilots to feign sickness and move about with hand over mouth and clutching stomachs. Having started with the Intelligence Office, he would then telephone AHQ and if the AOC was not available, would talk in flamboyant terms to the SASO. Afterwards the same Squadron Leader would transfer himself to 'my' chair and entertain any off-duty pilots with stories of his remarkable feats relating to his recent flying activity and history. My office now being full to capacity, I could stand about or go elsewhere. The places he was talking about we had been servicing for six or seven months at least. After one of these sessions I was told Warburton claimed he received a gong every six months. My previous experience of Royal Air Force Officers had been on a mainly courteous basis with modesty taking a large part in their recounting of experiences. As has been mentioned, I believed in keeping 'my' flight informed about what was happening and what would be expected of them and me by the Air Staff. All this changed with the advent of Warburton. Now nominated as Squadron Commander, he didn't move far from my office nor did he take any part in running the flight except to undertake sorties which appealed to him and which it seemed to us gave him the best chance of a good story for the AOC. The Senior Air Staff would seek out the CO of 69 Squadron to pass on important information to his PRU people in the flight. Unfortunately, that's where the information stayed and we were left in ignorance of quite relevant intelligence and instructions/orders. For instance, all the activity associated with the North African landings, both before and after the event.

It was one of these western sorties to the island of Sardinia – to Cagliari. It was my turn to do the midday sortie and Cagliari had come up. I had changed out of khaki shorts and shirt into my blue serge uniform, for flying, and contacted Met. and Control. Lugging parachute etc., I made my way to the aircraft and was settling myself into it when I became aware of the presence of Squadron Leader Warburton standing on the wing. 'Oh, Harry,' he said, 'I'm taking this trip.' You're to go down to Valletta and accompany Christine – his girl friend – to lunch on the *Brisbane Star.* He then said where Christine would be waiting and without further ado climbed into the aircraft as I vacated it. I changed again, out of heavy blue uniform, into khaki, found my bicycle and set off for Valletta to the address I had noted, and Christine.

The young woman, whom I assumed was Christine, opened the

door with apparent apprehension on seeing an unknown air force officer instead of her expected escort. After I had reassured her about the safety of Warburton, she invited the dusty cyclist inside to a cup of tea. Christine informed me that it was now too late for the lunch appointment. It was long past midday so as well as a cup of tea, she asked me if I would like a dash of Scotch in it. At the time, I thought it a very enterprising suggestion and the first time I had enjoyed such a combination. It was many years later that I met Captain Riley, the Master of the *Brisbane Star*, who said he had waited lunch for a very long time as I explained what had taken place.

It was also much later that I discovered what was happening in the western Mediterranean and how Warburton was playing his cards close to his chest. It was into October that he said to me that 'it had been decided' that if I would stay on until the New Year – I can't imagine what else I could do – I would be granted leave, (I think it was ten days), in Cairo and then I would go back to England for my greatly desired conversion onto Mosquito photographic reconnaissance. The Cairo bit was a mystery as it remains today. In every respect this was news to me, or should I say us, for as far as we knew, there was no tour laid down for us, the rank and file. We just went on until we dropped into the sea or if lucky, became a prisoner-of-war.

There was no further advice on the subject of leave and we continued very busily with our 'earlies and lates' on the Italian fleet whilst Warburton took aircraft and flew them, we/I didn't necessarily know where.

November arrived and there was now more winter weather in the form of cloud and precipitation to contend with, especially in our target areas. There were still the before first-light and last-light sightings required and on the tenth day of the month my second flight had disappeared under the hand of Squadron Leader Warburton, apparently to the western target of Sardinia, for which I had been briefing myself. On my own terms and to be fair to the others, that would mean another, third in a row, sortie before first light for me now that my last-light sortie had been taken by Warburton. I had become tired, not only of Warburton's boorish smug behaviour but the long series of before first-lights and last-lights was taking its toll. I found one of my pilots willing to trade with me to let me do his 'last light' so off I went, in this case to the Italian Naval base at Taranto. Also Messina and Augusta. I had now completed over 150 operational · sorties from Malta in the eight months or so. Arriving at Taranto, there was a lot of cloud and at various levels. I'd find a hole, then the harbour would be obscured by another layer. Heavy rain from other layers didn't improve matters nor did the Italian anti-aircraft gunners who were getting in a lot of heavy practice. After several circuits counting the battleships and cruisers, using my verticals as well as the oblique camera, with which this new aircraft was fitted, I vacated the area and made my way, climbing from under 8,000 feet on the way to Messina. There was a cruiser there, which I just had to sight, at Messina and their gunners too, were keen to deter me. Eventually, a hole in the cloud, at about 5,000 feet let me see it and note it. Next stop Augusta!

On my way past Mt Etna, I was climbing again for there were three cruisers there which had been confirmed in Augusta on previous thrice-daily sorties. They had moved over from Navarino in Greece where we had been watching them. Once again my altimeter began to unwind as I descended below the first layer of cloud, looking for a hole to observe the three cruisers. Another layer of cloud over the harbour saw me south of Augusta looking north through a hole in that cloud layer and my luck was in, for the moment. There were the three cruisers; I was free to go home. Now!

I had just rounded out, at 4,000 feet, and my speed was approximately 400 miles an hour. There was a loud crunching noise from the rear of the aircraft and the nose went violently down as in a bunt. Simultaneously, I had a glimpse of the Perspex windscreen distorting in front of me before I lost consciousness. I came to, outside the aircraft, falling freely through the air. I looked down as I felt the air rushing past my ears. My helmet had gone and there was a swirling turbulent circle of sea below where, presumably, the Spitfire had gone in. I looked down again and found the rip-cord misplaced down my body and although there didn't seem to be any urgency, I pulled it and the parachute opened with a jerk and I was in the sea.

In parachute drill, the recommended way to enter the water is to rotate a disc on the front of the quick release box so that on entering the water a blow with the fist will free the parachute. There had been no time for such action and on my landing in the sea, the parachute proceeded to pull me along like an aquaplane, further out to sea.

It was now so quiet with only the lapping of the waves to be heard. I was overcome with sorrow as I believed this was the end of my flying career. It was getting quite dark now on the water as I undid the dinghy pack which the lanyard, attached to my life-jacket, had pulled away from the parachute when I let it go. I was glad we had practised this sort of thing in swimming baths in the United Kingdom. Unfolding the dinghy, I found the CO_2 bottle and in no time the one-man craft was forming and when it did, I climbed in. This was before, in the development of these little one-man lifeboats, they had a cover to keep the occupant dry and mine proved to be an old model with no apron. As fast as I baled, the waves filled it up again. I gave that up and paddled in the direction of where I thought the shore would be – where the sun had set – the sky was lighter in that direction.

Because of injury from the hood when I was catapulted through it and breaking the Sutton harness, I could only see with one eye and there was some blood about, which was soon diluted with sea water. I was feeling very sorry for myself. This was 10 November 1942 and on the 8th, I had received a signal to the effect that I had been awarded the DFC. There had been no time to acquire and put up the ribbon and now in the cold, with my teeth chattering, I contemplated my rashness in taking on this flight to avoid working to my own rules of another third consecutive pre-dawn and last-light dual sortie day on the 11th of November, Armistice Day. My Dalton computer had survived with me so I unbuckled that from my leg and dropped it in the sea. I had lost all sense of time. My watch, which had been given to me by my grandmother for my 21st Birthday, had stopped and anyway now I could not see it. In those days RAF navigation watches were not issued to us but there were very good instrument panel clocks in the PR Spitfire which incorporated time of trip and stop watch facilities. Ideal for our navigation purposes.

In our earlier days on General and Photographic Reconnaissance in mid-Mediterranean with no airborne rescue services on our side, Les, Jo and I used to discuss having to contend with engine failure while out of range of our rescue launches but we did not decide the best moves in some of the, arguably, hopeless scenarios then existent. In the event, I had not had to cope with the decision, only the effect.

As I sat in the water with the waves washing over me, the only sound, I realised that back at base, they would be wondering where I had got to and then they would realise I would not be returning. With Frank Gillions, the first, I was now the second in our little unit who had failed to return. Both of us from New Zealand. I thought too, of a story John Tucker had told me. He was a Lieutenant in the Dorset Regiment who had been seconded to the Intelligence section at Luqa, along with another army officer, Lt Ian Gammidge, of the Buffs. Ian found fame after the war as a cartoonist in the London Press. John used to go sailing, solo, off Malta whenever the opportunity offered. One day he came across a German pilot sitting, like me now, in his K-type dinghy, off the coast of Malta where he had been surviving for about a week. I could understand why he did not put up any resistance to being rescued or at the same time being captured by an unarmed yachtsman. Regrettably, John Tucker lost his life later on when taking part in the invasion of Sicily.

CHAPTER EIGHT

POW – ITALY

S uddenly, in the gloom, I could make out a small steam vessel quite close. It pulled in alongside me and strong arms reached down and began lifting me up towards the deck and I, oddly, reached behind me and pulled the dinghy up too! They lay me down on the deck alongside the wheelhouse which was illuminated inside with electric lights. I had not been there very long before a sleek launch pulled alongside and I was transferred to this other vessel. Once on board, I was laid down on a stretcher this time. The only crew personnel of whom I was aware, was the coxswain, a medical man and a naval padre who asked me, in English, if I was a Roman Catholic. The medical naval man tied up my bleeding face and head and we then left the vicinity of the steamer and presumably set course for the Augusta Harbour heads. At the quayside steps I was unshipped on the stretcher and loaded like a tray of buns, into the waiting ambulance. The vehicle started up and we motored a short distance then stopped again. I lay there in the stationary ambulance for what seemed in excess of half an hour. I do not remember whether I was covered but I was still in my wet uniform with my teeth chattering. I was laid before an assembly of officers mainly Italian Navy, at a long table, with a central figure, whom I later learned, was the Admiral in Command at Augusta. He chaired proceedings and led most of the questions in English.

The Admiral said the Marine Artillery had shot me down. He remarked, 'Ah, New Zealand', reading my identity label. He went on to describe his being a pilot on board an Italian cruiser which he named and he had visited Wellington in that capacity, pre-war and that he had had a very good time. I was very pleased to hear that as I was virtually at their mercy. He directed various questions about what I was doing, what Squadron I belonged to and I gave the reply that I could only give my name, rank, which he knew, and number. To other questions, I gave similar replies and there was no pressure or 'arm twisting'. Eventually I was taken away on my stretcher to a barred-windowed room with a trestle bed in it. I was quite pleased when they stripped my wet clothes off and a doctor proceeded to examine me minutely. He was particularly careful about my injured head and face. I was surprised at my grazed shoulders and thighs where the aircraft harness had been before it broke with the force of my ejection. My head had apparently broken through the Perspex canopy and windscreen. The Italian doctor and his assistant bandaged me up after a sponge bath and then withdrew.

I was left with an armed guard in the room and after a while an orderly was admitted with a meal on a tray. It was a meal, the like of which I had not seen since I left England on the 1st of March. It was now November. Half a bottle of wine, some meat and salad and other items like bread roll etc., were spread before me. I toyed with this wonderful food but I didn't feel hungry. I suppose I was in a state of shock. The doctor had given me something in a glass which may have taken effect and even with a headache, I went to sleep. I noted, just before I slept, one guard in the lighted room with me, one outside the door and one outside the window looking in. I suggested to my inside man that I could do without the light to which I received a negative gesture. Sometime during the night, I woke to find two guards polishing off the meal I had failed to eat and they appeared to be enjoying it immensely. I went to sleep again.

The doctor came again next day and examined me thoroughly again. The Admiral followed and asked me how I was getting on, to which I replied, something like, 'Fine thanks'. While he was there, he asked me if I would like a bath or a shower – with my turban of bandages, I selected a bath. Eventually, I was escorted on my feet now, to a very pleasant bathroom with the three guards in place, as before, one inside the room, one on the door and another outside the window. I had a wonderful bath after which I was escorted back to bed in a pair of clean Italian pyjamas.

The doctor came in routinely each day and changed my dressings. After about three or four days, the Admiral came to visit again and this time he said, 'Tomorrow, you are going to Poggio Mirteto, up north'. To my further question he said that it was about an hour north of Rome. He added, 'As you pass Messina, you will be joined by an English Major'. Meanwhile, my uniform, with shirt and underclothes, had been returned, dried and folded. When I was about to leave my prison of a room, an orderly came in with a parcel of food. I looked in it and it seemed to be composed of two of what we know in New Zealand, as Vienna loaves stuffed with meat and salad. I said I didn't really need that. 'You take it', he said in English, with emphasis. It proved to be very wise counsel.

We left the room and waiting on one of the base roads was a tall dark blue limousine which reminded me strongly of the Hudson limousines which were used at one time as taxis, in New Zealand, circa early 1920s. They quite often had a silver vase containing flowers and elaborate blinds. This vehicle did not have those decorations but even now in 1942, it was very well preserved and the guard got into the back seat and patted alongside him for me to sit there with the corporal on the other side and off we drove to the railway station.

As we drove along the Naval base roads, Italian service families and some Naval men lined up to wave goodbye. Extraordinary! But I enjoyed it all the same! I waved back as if I was in a State procession. At the railway station I was escorted to a seat on the platform where immediately a crowd gathered around me and my two guards. They were just curious and inclined to be friendly to this foreign uniformed figure in blue with his head bandaged. After a while, the crowd was parted by a past-middle-aged man in a civilian navy blue double-breasted suit. 'Do you remember me?' he addressed me in English. I had to admit that I did not. 'You should do!' he added, 'I saved your life!' It was then that I realised he was the Master of the small steam vessel which had first come to my rescue. I believe I thanked him before he was swallowed up in the crowd. Soon, an Italian army *Tenente*, (Lieutenant) appeared, to take command of my party and perhaps he had had his instructions regarding the passage of our party to Rome, couched in terms resembling my instructions about taking my party from Bournemouth to Grangemouth, in Scotland. Whatever, he didn't look at all pleased with his task. The train came in and we, the four of us, took seats in a glassed-in compartment and the *Tenente* spoke to the Corporal who then stopped anyone else from entering. As we left the station I saw the blue limousine parked alongside the railway fence with the driver and another waving a last goodbye as we passed. At Messina, we were joined by another prisoner, as forecast by the Admiral at Augusta. I instantly recognised the new prisoner as Squadron Leader Payne, a Beaufighter pilot who was a relative newcomer to Luqa. I had seen the arrival of all the operational pilots who were currently operating there. Payne, being a 'new boy', looking at a new Air Force Station full of unfamiliar faces, it was not surprising that he showed no sign of recognising me. I greeted him but he ignored me until a long way into our journey. It was after we had crossed the Messina Straits and I had noticed I was under his scrutiny, that the 'thaw' started. He was glad to share my food and later revealed that that was his chief reason for being suspicious of me and also he saw that my injuries were not faked, as he had at first thought. He'd imagined I was a 'plant'. He then disclosed that he had been shot down near Trapani some days previously, and had had little or nothing to eat since – he was starving. I could well understand his feelings. After the treatment he'd had, to stumble across me, who'd been so well looked after and indeed, had been given food for the journey, it seemed hard for him to understand in the circumstances.

I don't remember much of that journey to the north, arriving at the Rome railway station in the morning, after an uncomfortable squirming and dozing night in our seats. Our three escorts guided us to a platform seat and the *Tenente* hovered around. As we sat there, we enquired about how long we would have to wait. Payne and I had finished our/my food on arrival so we were very hungry again long before midday. From what little we could extract in the way of information from the rather hostile *Tenente*, we would have to just sit there until the train left for Poggio Mirteto later in the afternoon. Some prospect!

An Italian *Majori* walked past, keenly observing our little party as we sat on. A little later, he came back and this time he spoke in French. Payne had a useful knowledge of the language and relayed to me that the Italian officer was a doctor and he was enquiring whether I would like my head dressings changed. I was moved to think it would relieve our situation of just sitting there and I said yes. Payne relayed this to the *Majori* who seemed pleased and approached the *Tenente*, who obviously wasn't. Mercifully, we did not understand the arguments, but the tone was unmistakable. At last the *Majori* won and we all moved back along the station, eventually arriving at what must have been a field dressing station. I had to take a seat while the medical people got to work, after which I felt very much more comfortable.

The *Tenente* and the Corporal and the others were making a move to go back to our platform when the Italian *Majori* asked Payne if we had eaten to which he replied, 'No, we have no money'. 'I'll pay'. said the *Majori* and the *Tenente* was hijacked into a deviation into a sort of NAAFI/YMCA where Payne and I polished off a wonderful dish of minestrone with very good sized pieces in it. Then, and only then, did the *Majori* go on his way. What a kind man!

Eventually, our train came in and we were escorted to a carriage for the 'hour north of Rome', to Poggio Mirteto. On arrival at P.M. we had to alight on the track away from the station – the train being surrounded by armed guards with fixed bayonets! We were bustled into a closed van which moved off as soon as the back doors were closed. Squadron Leader Payne and I were eventually in the same room with no outside windows. There was a guarded corridor, open to the weather, along which we proceeded to the bathroom with one of the guards. As it had been disclosed, this was an interrogation centre so we were both careful about our conversation, especially after reading a printed notice near the door, containing (Italian) regulations for prisoners-of-war. We noticed a very small pencilled line between the printing – 'Beware of microphones in ceiling'. Study of the ceiling when the wind blew revealed a small section of the scalloped surface finish which moved slightly up and down suggesting a hollow beneath.

We were both taken away separately to be interrogated by an English-speaking civilian. In my case, he asked all the routine questions about my duties which I parried with my usual non-committal name, rank and number. At the end of the interview, the interrogator said he had no liking for his job and that he would be leaving it soon. The *Maracello*, (Warrant Officer), who was the most senior service person we encountered at this stage, had quite a lot to say in English; this included offering us extras to our meagre rations and cigarettes. These extras were to be charged to our banking accounts through the Red Cross. I discovered later that these extras and cigarettes were issued free to PoWs by the Red Cross through the 'parcel' system.

Eventually, Squadron Leader Payne disappeared and I too was despatched to a PoW camp. The Italians, unlike the Germans, segregated their war prisoners by nationality, whereas the Germans did it by Service, i.e. Navy, guarded by *Kriegsmarine*, Air Force, guarded by *Luftwaffe*, and Army, by the *Wehrmacht*. So, being under Italian jurisdiction I was allocated to *Campo* 47, at Modena on the Lombardy Plains in Central Northern Italy.

On arrival at the gate in the late evening, after my escort had formally handed me over to the Italian camp administration, I was met inside the compound by the camp adjutant, who was Lieutenant Sir de Villiers Graaf of the South African Army. It was now the 27th of November 1942, my 26th birthday. The Adjutant explained to me that he had been unable to accommodate me in the New Zealand block as he had hoped because 'they' had told him they had no room for me. After taking my particulars, he accompanied me to a marble floored block divided laterally into door-less rooms. I was introduced to all who were still awake and interested and given a trestle bed on the edge of the main passageway which ran from the central front door to the back end where the latrines and washrooms were situated.

The South Africans showed a lively but polite interest in my arrival and on the spot, had a 'whip round' for my comfort as I only had a piece of soap and a tooth brush given to me by the Admiral at Augusta. However, I was soon attired in a pair of pyjamas, home-made from an Italian palliasse. The brown and cream stripes went round and round and looked like a prison uniform. Someone produced a small square of towelling then a razor and soon I was relatively well equipped, so I, too, slept.

In the morning I was given a rundown by my South African friends of what was expected in the way of roll-call, – then off to the end of the passageway for bathroom duties. Then followed 'breakfast' in the dining block. This consisted of a little loaf of bread, the size of a modern bread roll, at a table at which I had been allocated a seat next to two South Africans who were members of that country's Police Regiment. One of them, Paxton, was serving anything which came in bulk such as coffee/tea or the main course at dinner.

Then back to the barrack-room where there were lots of interesting discussions going on. Young Lt Schofield was a pilot I then met, who had been flying Kitty- or Tomahawks.

Captain Botha, DSO, was the Room Commander. The main body of the Army officers in my vicinity had been captured at the fall of Tobruk, when their General Klopper surrendered in mid-summer. It was now winter, in northern Italy and their summer uniform was quite inadequate for the temperatures prevailing.

They were nearly all wearing long white Red Cross underwear beneath their khaki drill shorts. The roll-call was a time of direct comparison between the two nationalities and their wardrobes. The New Zealand Army were all well dressed, as befitted their longer period of captivity whilst my new companions were very lightly clothed in a variety of summer garments. Nevertheless, the South Africans were extremely generous with any spares. Later that morning I was invited outside to meet the New Zealand prisoners who swarmed around me and fired questions at me endlessly. These questions took the form of what school had I attended and where did I live in New Zealand? What was my occupation pre-war? What did my father do for a living? How much did I earn pre-war? When did I join up for war service? Did I know 'John Brown' or 'David Smith?' etc. Did I play rugby? All these questions plied with an intensity unmatched by the Italian interrogators of earlier experience. One among the crowd told me he was Flt Lt Campbell, who had been flying a Blenheim and had been shot down in the Adriatic near Yugoslavia. He told me later that they were mainly New Zealand Army and suspicious of my story of operating alone in the Mediterranean: they perhaps being used to operating in large army bunches, didn't understand. Whatever, the New Zealand PoWs then left me alone with my new found South African friends which Campbell said they considered the prudent way to go, since no one knew me!

I was still wearing the same clothes in which I had landed in the sea on the 10th of November and it was now the 28th. My clothes had been dried but probably not washed. My footwear was still my wool-lined flying boots so I was extremely grateful when my room-mates had another spontaneous 'whip round' for a shirt and an old pair of rope-soled sneakers and a pair of socks to wear with them. Ultimately, I was issued with a pair of Red Cross boots and some underwear as well as a British Army greatcoat from the same source. Apart from standing about in the freezing wind on roll-call, the greatcoat was a marvellous addition for the bed as a blanket.

My immediate South African neighbours, around my bed space, continued to prove very friendly and helped in any way they could. Athletic and well-built Fritz Wagner, of a South African Rifle Regiment and a little Irish South African tank officer, O'Donovan, who was trying to grow hair on his prematurely bald pate, were the closest in location. Others like Lawson, always working on some scheme and a great sportsman as well as a mathematician – Afrikaner Oostacen, and room commander, Dane Botha, with Michael Sedgewick, completed my side of the half room. The latter, tall, slim as a reed and a South African pilot, Lt Schofield, from another room were my particular friends.

At Modena, my bed was on the edge of the passage way with the pedestrian population of the block passing to and fro to the ablutions as well as traffic to other bed spaces and rooms. The ablutions area contained marble appointed bathrooms and lavatories. The latter types were common enough in Italy but novel to us at first. Effectively, it was a stream of water running beneath a hole which was between two foot-rests. For vital bodily functions, one suspended the body over the hole by squatting with the feet on the foot-rests.

The South African uniform, in the main, featured an orange/red tab on the epaulettes, which I understand indicated the wearer was a volunteer who would serve outside the boundaries of South Africa, in North Africa. This, I believe, was negotiated by Field Marshal Smuts, to show willingness of South Africa to help the Allied cause. In the main, we all dressed as close as possible to the correct dress for our rank and service.

I remember one prisoner-of-war however, who wore a khaki battledress with two gold stripes and because, when I asked him what he had been flying and the reply was a Swordfish, I at first thought he was a Navy man – especially as he wore a full beard. It transpired he was a Flight Lieutenant in the RAF. He was one of the four of us at our dining table.

I had a very happy association with the South Africans in my isolation which continued throughout my time at Modena Campo. A day's programme began with the morning roll-call about 8 o'clock. There were various bugle calls made by the Italians in their divided-off compound, outside the wire, but within the outside high wall, which had significance for them but not for us. The Italian orderly officer wore a magnificent sash over his shoulder with tassles hanging down his side. The Italian camp officer was usually an Alpini with the high, decorated, felt hat of that Regimental unit. The Italian officers' everyday uniform, was much more ornate than anything we knew. Everybody lined up in threes along the central road in the compound and the camp officer counted the threes in company with our Adjutant Lieutenant, Sir Villiers Graaf. There were three main blocks of buildings in use. One block exclusively for New Zealand officers, one for South African officers and one which was used for catering, i.e. cooking and dining.

Red Cross parcels were issued on the basis of one to a prisoner each week. At Modena, the parcels were opened by the catering department run by a New Zealand officer who took out the meats and stews and such-like items. He made up a weekly menu which was displayed outside for us to drool over. Likewise, he took in the Italian issue rations which were fairly basic like pasta and vegetables of minimum quantity to be blended by his skill into very appetising combinations. Once a week, a meal that was greatly looked forward to, was Pasta Chuta. This special meal was made from a combination of items from Red Cross parcels and pasta and for once made us feel replete.

At the end of the compound was a building which was mainly used for recreation with tables and chairs and a table tennis area. Like the marble floors, wine is a characteristic of Italy and there was a *vino* issue to the prisoners like us. We somehow paid for this through the Red Cross and our bank accounts held in our base countries. There was a camp bank and accounting system run by PoW officers and audited, of course, by the Italians. The *vino* was not available for general sale but was issued by the production of a ration ticket and at the recreation building. Each recipient took along his tin mug for his portion of Marsala once a week – *Vin Ordinaire* was available a little more liberally.

There were a few other ranks in the camp who had volunteered for such jobs as kitchen, dining and sick bay duties. In the dining-rooms which were in the same style and arrangement as the blocks in which we slept, there were tables seating four and at breakfast there was a plate at each place with a small loaf of bread, like a bun, which was issued each day.

Theoretically, we received a Red Cross parcel once a week and as mentioned, these were deployed through the catering department but in times of wartime stress, the interval between parcels became greater. The packages contained cigarettes too. Fifty in English parcels – 60 or 70 in an American one and similarly, in Canadian. There were no cigarettes in the New Zealand food parcels – I think they came separately – but sometimes issued on the same basis as the English ones at 50 per week. These New Zealand parcels were not the most popular because the meat content was Bully beef, a mass of skin and tubes, whereas the Canadian and US deliveries contained Spam and similar manufactured products. The English parcels had a mixture of things including stews of steak and kidney which were very well received. Portions of dried egg in tins and butter were popular too. The tinned butter from New Zealand was always rancid and un-usable. The butter and spreads were issued individually whilst things like egg powder, stews and meat products were served in bulk at the table mainly at evening meals. Tea, from the parcels, was the beverage.

After meals, we adjourned to our barrack blocks. There were pre-arranged lectures, including language classes, PT, games of touch rugby, soccer etc., tenniquoit and volleyball. As part of escape activity, I eventually became involved in map-making. The Italians were very shy about allowing us maps and if they found them, even in books and newspapers, they confiscated them so it behove us to make maps of our own. We would laboriously make them from small scale ones, which somehow we had acquired, into a large scale suitable for finding a way across country after escaping.

I laboured under the direction of a South African officer who had been something like a cartographer in civilian life. We would work at a table in a passageway by a window, in the front of the barrack block and by prior arrangement, we would be alerted to the danger of advancing Italians, by fellow prisoners. We had a very good view from where we worked, of the gate and pathways which led to us. These were escape maps which we made and each map was an individual enlargment of the small ones. We didn't even dream of the day when photo or electronic copying would be available.

Among the lecturers, was a South African pilot who had been flying Ju 52s in an airline capacity. The *Luftwaffe* used amazing numbers of these aircraft so the pilots amongst us took notes of cockpit arrangements, handling and starting details in case we ever had the chance of taking one or helping someone else to do so. There was another pilot, a Rhodesian, who had been one of the juniors on a Sunderland flying boat when it had been attacked by two CR42s, (Italian biplane fighters), which had picked off one of its four engines and then another of its engines forcing it to alight on the sea off Tobruk. Two Italian destroyers appeared in the vicinity but did not come close. However, one of the other junior pilots took the aircraft axe and hacked a hole in the bottom to avoid the destroyers capturing the Sunderland intact. In the event, the Italian destroyers stayed at a distance and to avoid the flying boat sinking before the crew could be rescued, the crew had to strip off their clothes to plug the hole! Inevitably, they were all captured. The narrator, a Rhodesian, was at the time of relating the event, quartered in the New Zealand block at Modena.

In one of the rooms located on the front of their dormitory block, the New Zealand officers had inaugurated a bank and record office where they noted new arrivals, in Campo 47, and all their particulars. They also issued the coupons for the distribution of the wines. The *vin ordinaire* was inclined to blacken the teeth of those who had traded extra coupons. This 'trading' was likely to take place on special occasions such as birthdays and other anniversaries.

Of the various lectures, which were in full swing at the date of my arrival, I opted to join the French language class but the lecturer thought that without my having a basic grounding at school, it would be too difficult and advised against it.

Escorted walks were sometimes arranged for the afternoons and these were greatly appreciated events. The participants would line up in threes along the centre roadway which led from the central main gate down to the bottom of the compound. Personnel were marshalled in a similar manner to the roll-call. We would be counted in threes, with the officiating Italian officer in front and another Italian at the other end of the file, at the rear. The 'private' style Italian soldiers, armed with rifles, would fall in on each side of the prisoners and we would proceed through the gate and down the straight roads on the Lombardy Plains. In winter time the green vegetation of crops etc., had disappeared leaving only the very black soil. The roads were very straight with open ditches at the side. Occasionally, a motor truck would pass us and sometimes, too, there would be an Italian tenor singing his heart out on the back of the vehicle.

Eventually, the Italian officer in charge of the walk would call a halt and the whole column would about-face. We would then proceed back along the way we had come. These walks would occupy something like an hour but it was only an estimation, for my watch had been ruined in the sea.

There was an interesting escape on one of these walks. At the time, our Senior British Officer, (SBO), was a South African. One day, he and two others disappeared and although the Italians conducted a full scale search and investigation, they could not ascertain *how* they had disappeared. Several weeks later, as a member of the escape workers, I was approached, mainly because of my height, (6ft 1″ in my shoes), to take a part in the final departure of those three. The wardrobe department had obtained or constructed, three sets of civilian clothes, with shoes etc. to match. As well as the civilian clothes, the escape industry had cleverly constructed collapsible khaki battledresses to cover the civilian clothes. The special battledress garments were held together with strings which could be withdrawn whereupon the whole uniform fell away. I was detailed to fall-in with other tall officers, in files of three, in front and behind the three escapees, to mask what was about to happen, from the eyes of the guards.

At a signal, the group of threes, both ahead and behind the escapers, tended to crowd the nearest guard. At the same time, the strings were pulled and the outside khaki garments grabbed and disposed of on our adjacent persons. The escapers turned left and at the edge of the column, turned left again and the approaching guard was confronted with three civilians on the crowded edge of the ditch, going the other way! We tidied up our clothing dispersal and proceeded to the turn round point of the walk. There seemed to be no panic and so we arrived back at the camp gate in normal manner. The file of three escaping had another clever aspect too. If we were counted in threes on return, there could be an argument that a miscount had taken place, on leaving – one file too many. If it was still in doubt, count the whole camp again! The camp total would be the same as when we left.

In the event, nothing such as a recount took place, as the whole walk had been so straight-forward and normal and sedately conducted, we were marched straight in and dispersed. Later that day, the Modena railway station-master rang up the Italian Commandant to say that he thought he had one of the Allied prisoners down there, who had escaped from Modena PoW camp. The Commandant is reputed to have replied, 'No you haven't, we haven't lost anybody!' So they conducted a full roll-call which revealed no one missing. The station master then divulged that his captive had admitted that he had come from our camp which was a huge embarrassment to the Italian Commander.

It transpired that this prisoner, after successfully getting away from the walk with the other two, had encountered some muddy ground as he made his way separately to the railway station. While he waited on the platform, some children had commented on his muddy footwear which was in marked contrast to the rest of his clothes. He was not sufficiently conversant with the Italian language to talk his way out of it and the resulting commotion attracted attention and eventually the station-master took a hand in the affair. After this, we had incessant roll-calls and searches.

It was thought that one of the other two eventually got away but the upheaval of the Italian capitulation and evacuation from Modena, made details like that, uncertain. Our SBO, meanwhile, had become Lt-Col. Shuttleworth of the New Zealand Army. I don't recall any other escapes from Modena until the end came.

We all hoped we would get away and that would be when or if the Italians capitulated. Such hopes were pinned on that being when the Allies landed on the mainland in the south. That release possibility was not to be capable of being used until September 1943.

Eventually, when that happened, most of us wanted to be off at once but our New Zealand SBO told us to stay put until the Allies arrived because if we went out we would probably be captured and taken to Germany. Also, the Italians were still sniping from the sentry towers at people trying to sneak away. Then we thought we heard distant gunfire but it turned out to be only someone shifting potatoes in the bin! Rumours about the Allied advance were rife but none of our people appeared and we learned to our sorrow that there was nothing closer than the landing at Anzio after all.

The New Zealand Flight Lieutenant who had flown Blenheims and could speak Italian, had invited me to go with him when the 'balloon went up' which I thought was a great idea! However, in the event, when the New Zealand SBO said to us 'You can go', I couldn't find the Flight Lieutenant anywhere and had to assume he had gone without me. From that moment of my despair, I realised it was too late for me to get out of the camp. The Italians were discarding their uniforms in favour of civilian clothes and making off and disappearing into the countryside. It was a period of confusion for us.

Route taken as PoW across Europe

Les Colquhoun outside our sleeping quarters at Siggiewi Signal Station in 1942.

ABOVE: The office desk! Writing my photographic report on the Spit's wingtip in March 1942. The camera staff are waiting to take the cameras' magazines to Valletta.

BELOW: Outside the Intelligence Office at Luqa in 1942. *Left to right:* Lieutenant John Tucker, Dorset Regiment, the author, Lieutenant Ian Gammidge, 'The Buffs' and Sergeant Les Colquhoun, RAF.

ABOVE: Jim Berrett, ex RAFVR, who was a member of 69 Squadron operating Marylands from Malta in 1941 and prime mover in encouraging me to write this autobiography.

Luqa in late 1942. Lieutenant John Tucker of the Dorset Regiment, seated and Pilot Officer Jo Dalley, later Group Captain. Regretfully, John Tucker lost his life during the invasion of Sicily the following year.

'This photo I treasure, as almost everyone who provided the intelligence for the worst period of the siege is included.' Group Captain J.O. Dalley, OBE, DFM. *Back row left to right:* HQ photographic officer, Jo Dalley, PR pilot, the author, unknown. *Front row left to right:* Les Colquhoun, PR pilot, Hershell, HQ photo interpreter, Colvin, HQ photo interpreter, unknown.

Naples
Harbour
1942.

Tripoli in 1942.

These five photographs were taken at the height of the bombing in Malta. The one above shows Valletta harbour under attack in 1942 and the other four indicate the horrific battering that the island took from the air.

A common sight on a sparkling Mediterranean in 1942.

This burning ship was photographed by the author on 17 August 1942, after it had been attacked by RAF Beauforts.

Personalkarte I: Personelle Angaben *Coldbeck H. G.*

Beschriftung der Erkennungsmarke
Nr. *3400*

Kriegsgefangenen-Stammlager: Stalag Luft 3

Lager: *OFLAG II A*

Name: *COLDBECK*

Vorname: *Henry Gift*

Geburtstag und -ort: *27.11.16 Neuseeland*

Religion: *C of E*

Vorname des Vaters:

Familienname der Mutter:

Staatsangehörigkeit: **NEUSEELAND**

Dienstgrad: *F/Lt.*

Truppenteil: *RNZAF* Kom. usw.:

Zivilberuf: Berufs-Gr.:

Matrikel Nr. (Stammrolle des Heimatstaates) *NZ 405235*

Gefangennahme (Ort und Datum): *9.9.43 Sizilien*

Ob gesund, krank, verwundet eingeliefert:

Des Kriegsgefangenen

Lichtbild

Nähere Personalbeschreibung

Grösse	Haarfarbe	Besondere Kennzeichen:
183	*blond*	*Res. Adr. C/. 432 Gloucester St. Christchurch*

des rechten Zeigefingers

Name und Anschrift der zu benachrichtigenden Person in der Heimat des Kriegsgefangenen

48

MRS. E. M. CAMPBELL
44 ST HELIERS ST.
CHRISTCHURCH. N.Z.

The German personal identification card which recorded the author's POW history.

The old order changeth – a Meteor puts a Spitfire into the background in 1947. The author looks on.

The author flying Mosquito PR Mk 34 'OT'. This aircraft was the fastest version of the Mosquito and was capable of 422 mph in level flight. It had a range of 3,500 miles at 315mph at an altitude of 30,000 feet. The photo was taken in 1949 whilst the author was based at RAF Benson.

OC 'F' Flight at RAF Feltwell between 1950 and 1953. Instructors and pupils.

Chapter Nine

PoW – Germany

Whilst all this running about and confusion was going on, in came the Germans who set up a machine-gun post in the parade square. Eventually, word came that we were to form up with what we could carry and then we were marched off down the street guarded by armed Germans, to the main railway station, where a line of covered cattle trucks awaited our arrival. Just cattle trucks – no seats and no straw. Just a wooden floor and not devoid of animal droppings. Fifty prisoners to a truck. The door was slammed shut – no food – no provision for anything, I recall. We passed other trains with ranks of open trucks, in the hot sun, which were full of Italians. The Italian prisoners were excreting in cardboard boxes, if they had any, because they were not allowed off the train. They were shot if they misbehaved in the slightest way. We understood, through our looking through the small foot square ventilators at each corner of the cattle trucks, that they were Italians who had remained loyal to Italy.

We kept stopping for long periods and without food or water being supplied. We ascertained, eventually, that we were travelling through the Brenner Pass. That section of our miserable journey ended at Innsbruck where the doors were opened and we all jumped or fell out onto the track adjacent to an enormous PoW Camp at Moosburg. We soon discovered the thousands who inhabited this crude human stockyard, were Russians, Serbs, Croats and many other nationalities who were being very badly treated. The Germans would put a 44-gallon drum with something resembling pig swill, into their compound and these poor creatures would have to get it out as best they could – with hands or anything they had. If the drum overturned in the struggle to get some they would scrape it up off the ground.

We thought ourselves fortunate, so far, not to have been treated like that. Nevertheless, eating was a luxury to be provided from our own packs and once a day the Germans supplied us with some gruel in our tin mugs which we were wise to have always carried with us.

The next move was the cattle truck train again but now we were in Germany and we trucked across the state to Strasbourg, in Alsace Lorraine. We had had a particularly long time closed in without being able to relieve ourselves and as soon as the guards would permit, a line of prisoners were squatting beside the train obeying the call of nature. A *Wermacht* officer came screaming along shouting, 'Get them out of here, get them out of here, there'll be a mountain of . . .' This was happening alongside the platform of a highly in-use railway station at Strasbourg.

Our quarters at Strasbourg turned out to be some large, long rooms which were situated end-on to a moat devoid of water. These long rooms were 'furnished' with two lengthwise shelves, something like vegetable shelves, sloping towards the front. One shelf above the other. On each shelf were large artificial hessian bags filled with wood wool, which served as mattresses. I was glad to find I was on a top shelf because, in no time, the woodwool started to disintegrate through the hessian-type stuff and to shower onto the unfortunates on the lower shelves.

The next move, and we were still the complete Modena complement, New Zealand and South Africa, Army, Navy and Air Force, was back into the cattle trucks and on to Viensburg. This camp looked a bit more civilised and we soon found out that the Army Officers' component of our number would be staying, while the Air Force would be siphoned off to another camp which proved to be *Stalag Luft* 3 at Sagan in Upper Silesia.

On arrival at *Stalag Luft* 3, our party was marched through the pine forests to an enormous clearing where there were four or five camps within a large outer *Voorelager*. Through this and up to the main gate of the North Compound, (as we found out later it was called), where a large group of Air Force prisoners-of-war, (*Kriegsgefangener*), waited to see if they knew any of the newcomers.

I was immediately approached by an officer whom I recognised as one who had been the flight sergeant pilot of the Anson at RAF Benson. He was then the NCO pilot who had had the difficulty with his navigational matters. He greeted me warmly and I greeted him by name and asked him what he was doing there, although I had my own ideas, on the basis of his history as a navigator. He replied to the effect that he had been tiring of flying the Anson, as a staff pilot and he had asked the Wing Commander if he could transfer to PRU. The Wing Commander authorised him a trial sortie, as it happened, in a brand new Spitfire with loaded cameras, to photograph specific targets along the south coast of England and other particular places, inland within our territory.

Off he went and climbed up to his briefed altitude but in so doing, he passed over some cloud and rather lost track of his whereabouts – not to worry, there was the coast below. There was, however, still some doubt in his mind about where he was on the coast and as he came down below the cloud, he could see flak towers. No one had mentioned flak towers on the south coast of England. Conveniently, an airfield with runways appeared underneath, so he decided to land and in his time honoured way, to find out. A motorcycle and side-car joined him, after landing and he noticed, as the crew signalled him to stop, with their submachine-guns, that they were wearing coal-scuttle type helmets. He was taken into custody and the brand new PR Spitfire, in perfect order, was in enemy hands. He thought I should have been more sympathetic towards his predicament. There is more!

He then told me that he had the Germans bluffed. He said, 'I've got "barbed wire psychosis," and they agree'. 'I'll be going home soon.' 'The members of the Protecting Power are coming to see me.' Sure enough, the Swiss Protecting Power gave him his 'ticket' to go home and we all had several more years behind the wire to serve, as he gleefully waved us goodbye!

Sagan is situated in Upper Silesia, on the western side of Poland, and *Stalag Luft* 3, on the site of a felled pine forest with stumps and furrows still in place in the sandy earth. The sand under the 'top soil' was a bright yellow a long way down. Quite good for tunnelling. We were now allocated a room in long wooden blocks, probably pre-fabricated with tarred paper on the roof with a wooden lining and floor, both in natural un-decorated form. Double tiered bunks – the bottom ones inhabited already – so it was the top one for we late comers. Later on, with a greatly increased population, the two-tier bunks were increased to three tiers. The top one's occupant could easily touch the ceiling.

I was at *Luft* 3 from the latter part of 1943 until after Christmas, 1944. Things were very different at this camp from the Italian type. For instance, the Germans, unlike the Italians, did not object to our having maps and charts. I did a second class navigator's course there, which involved maps, charts, astro charts and tables as well as weather maps. One of our lecturers was a Meteorological Officer who had 'gone along for the ride', and the aircraft he was 'riding' in was shot down. He was a fully qualified man with a degree and a splendid lecturer, as indeed, was the navigation officer. He used to set us the task of working up position lines from tables and previously recorded shots. We, that is, the few of us taking the navigation and meteorological courses, had, from time-to-time, to sit exams set by the lecturers.

Soon after arrival at Sagan, we were given a recruiting lecture by members of the escape organisation which led me to understand they were recruiting would-be tunnellers which I did not receive with much enthusiasm. Granted, there was an obligation on all of us to escape, whenever we could. There was, however, the Italian experience where there was an excellent chance of success with the countryside not wholeheartedly unfriendly and our exit had been denied! The best part of a year had been spent looking forward to the Italian capitulation and the possibility of rejoining a combatant force of our own. After all the chances I had had to pass up it seemed farcical, after the hungry weeks, the numerous cattle truck journeys and other privations, to go down on a claustrophobic tunnelling job. Anyway, I joined up with the security organisation and was given a team of my fellows to watch the gate in a sort of duty pilot role. Each time an officer of the German forces, or a 'ferret', (they wore blue overalls with an army belt), entered, I logged them and they were deleted on the account as they went out again. If an officer and two ferrets were in the camp, at any given time, a state of alarm existed and all vulnerable activity was warned on pre-arranged radius lines, from the gate. We tried to make these movements as least noticeable as possible for there were map-makers, tunnellers, tailors and forgers of documents who had to fold up and hide their work until the danger of detection passed. If they, the 'Goons', as the guards were dubbed, went out and the alarm relaxed back to normal, we maintained the watch until relieved.

In this connection when we went on *Apel* (roll-call) in the morning, it behove us to put everything we wanted to keep, treasures like bits of tin, a stone, (useful for tin bashing), wire, string, extra knives, any tools, hidden away out of sight. Whilst most times this may not have been necessary, we just never knew when we would return from *Apel* to find our hut guarded and out of bounds until the search was finished in an hour or so's time and our little treasures gone.

We had a secret radio which operated daily to listen in to, and to have transcribed, the BBC news. Specially appointed readers would go to various huts and the hut security people would conduct a search of loft space, under-floor space of each room and while this reading was underway, others would sight along the walls from each end, to note any agent or other person leaving or arriving. When all was clear, the news reader would read the news in the centre of the central passageway whilst the security people kept watch, from the end and central room windows. Most of us were extremely interested in what our main leaders had to say but none absorbed us more than Winston Churchill, whose forecasts, we noted, were the most likely to be fulfilled. It cheered everybody up no end, when the possibility of the Second Front became a reality on D-Day. We could compare the BBC detail of events with the German newspaper versions.

There were two water closets at the end of the hut and these were reserved for night use only, i.e. after the outside hut doors had been locked by the guards for the night. Anyone outside after this lock up was liable to be shot on sight and some, unhappily, were. The daytime latrines were somewhat crude affairs, consisting of a long open concrete tank with a lengthwise rail suspended over it on each side for the occupants to sit on. From time-to-time, a very elderly man would drive a horse-drawn circular tube wooden tank vehicle into the lager and pump out the contents of the concrete tank and cart it away. There were attempted escapes by means of this vehicle which was odoriferous in the extreme.

The two water closets were quite normal affairs but one was permanently out of bounds. It was universally assumed to be something to do with the secret radio. Some room stoves had been re-engineered to cover manhole access to a tunnel entrance which had been 'drilled' down through the concrete stove foundation to the ground below.

The stoves in each room were fairly big, free-standing affairs based on concrete, as referred to above. There was a small ration of a few briquettes to the rooms which also had to suffice for a coal-fired stove in the hut 'kitchen' to cook *the* meal of the day in the evening. A roster was drawn up and each room had approximately twenty minutes' time for the room 'cook' to boil things such as vegetables on the top and or something in the oven. This might be crushed biscuits made into a sort of cake. Potatoes were scrubbed and eaten, skins and all. Perhaps, for a special occasion, or a particular dish, they would be peeled after the scrubbing and the peelings saved and fried.

Each room had a tall jug like a coal hod, in which we used to carry water. In winter's cold, especially, we would have one of these jugs full of water ready to put on the stove when the cooking roster had been completed. This water would warm up enough for a stand-up wash down, on the concrete and drained floor of the washroom, where the basins were.

With such a small ration of fuel in large ceramic-type stoves, the allowance of heat tended to be absorbed by the stove construction itself. Most stoves were 're-engineered' by the inmates of the rooms so that the briquettes were in closer proximity to the metal top, which radiated the meagre heat available, to the room. Another modification was to the concrete chimney. In fact, a new chimney was constructed with the ubiquitous KLIM tins. (Milk, spelled backwards). These came in the Canadian and US Red Cross parcels, and when joined bottomless and end to end they made tubes of any length, to serve as the chimney nearest the heat source, joining the real chimney only after most of the heat had been radiated into the room.

All rooms had some sort of organisation to deal with the limited food available, the fuel supply and the dissemination of news and orders etc. The officer nominated in charge, was commonly known as the Room *Führer*. Then there was the cupboard *Führer*. He received the bulk supply and issued them to the cook of the day or week, or whatever time the room cook had agreed to do the duty. The cook served the meals in exact portions, at pre-arranged meal times which were in accordance with the stove roster. Now and again the stove was running behind time and those cooks, lower down the roster, would be fretfully hanging about the kitchen, trying to will things to go faster, so that he could placate his clientele in his room. Short cuts, to speed things along, like reserving another cook's potato water, were fairly commonplace. Our captors supplied the briquettes for the fire.

In our hut there was a Wing Commander Hull, nominally in charge. He occupied a single room at the end of the corridor and he kept a fairly benign, overall eye on things. He would attend Hut Commander meetings with the Senior British Officer, who in our case, was a Group Captain Massey, who had been injured in the leg, when he came down. Eventually he was repatriated. A very popular officer.

Various senior Wing Commanders used to deputise for the Group Captain if he was unwell or for any other reason he did not appear on parade, *Apel*, etc. Our *Luftwaffe* Lager Officer, was *Hauptman* Peber who claimed he was an Austrian. He and the *Oberfeldwebel* did the counting on 'roll-call' each day; Peber in front, with the *Oberfeldwebel* at the rear end of each file of three. They both conducted themselves correctly with very good humour and Peber, anyway, had a good command of the English language.

At some time in the life of the camp compound, permission had been obtained from the camp commandant, to establish a theatre. Red Cross plywood boxes, originally containing Red Cross parcels, had been fashioned into seats which, because, of the design, proved very comfortable for the duration of a show, put on by the PoWs. The roles of the female players had to be taken by the younger officers who sometimes, being goodlooking teenagers, with make-up on and legs shaved, were very convincing females. One member of the hut took such an interest in these theatre players, that he earned the nickname of 'Homo'. Those were the days when the word 'gay' was unknown to most of us anyway.

There were numerous actors on our camp stage who were to achieve great prominence on the world stage afterwards. Peter Butterworth, Lewis Casson, John Le Mesurier are a few of the names which come to mind, from those among us who entertained us in various of the well-known shows of the time. For a presentation like *The Importance of Being Earnest*, there was a box office where seats had to be pre-booked. There was also a special night when the Group Captain was host to the German Camp Commandant and his *aides-de-camp*.

It was important that the theatre be maintained in its flourishing style as it was such an undercover workshop for escape activity. All 'hollow spaces' around the camp such as under the theatre seats, sloping floors etc., were places where things could be hidden. The costume department was a great front for escape clothing, too. The whole camp must have been an absolute hive of activity, for the quality of the shows was remarkable, to say nothing of the excellence of the escape products which were, it seems, truly amazing. Forgers and tailors excelled.

Bridge playing attracted a great following. I believe many reached a very high standard of play. They certainly had endless practice, day after day, and the post-mortems went on in the darkened hut, far into the night, sometimes, inevitably, to the irritation of non-players. Gymnastics used to be a popular pastime and had quite a following. Mindy Blake, from New Zealand, in the RAF, who was Wing Commander Flying at Portreath, during my tour there, with 66 Squadron, was one of the leading exponents of this exercise and quite often drew a crowd of would-be adherents, as spectators. The Wooden Horse story of escape, is a well-known one from our neighbouring East Compound. Softball was a game I found myself involved in, becoming the pitcher for our team in the competitions and leagues etc. Here, too, in softball, the Canadians were very prominent as they were in ice-skating. In winter, in Upper Silesia, it was very cold but to put the freezing daytime temperatures to good use, we were able to make skating rinks simply by building up low walls, say six inches high, around a flat area and flooding it with a layer of water. When that layer of water froze, another layer was applied and so on until a good thick layer of smooth ice was formed on the ground. The Canadians were to the fore in this sport, but all nationalities took part and the supply of ice skates was the only limiting factor.

There was a large RAF Polish contingent, which occupied a whole hut to themselves. They were the best dressed officers in the camp and they maintained a tidy reticence as well.

Being an entirely air force population in the camp, it was natural that the exercise path on the perimeter, which hundreds of feet trod every day, would be known as the circuit. The path which the feet had formed was just inside the trip wire and that was about twelve feet from the fence of the compound. The general warning was that the sentries on foot and in the elevated box tower, would shoot at anyone going over the trip wire. If an object such as a ball went over, it was necessary to make arrangements with the guards to recover it. Our hut being on the outer corner of the camp, provided a constant review of the camp population as they trudged by in a left hand rotation, (anti-clockwise), as it followed the extremities of our world of that time.

Further comparisons with the Italian camp at Modena, were the wooden buildings which were in a group on one side of the compound, whereas in Italy, they were of stone, around the perimeter, with a tall stone fence all around the camp so that it was impossible to see anything of life outside. Here, at Sagan, whether we liked it or not, we saw and heard labour and army groups singing lustily as they progressed through the forest, as well as the various motorised and horse-drawn traffic. In Italy, as already mentioned, some rationed wine could be purchased and enjoyed along with conversation and discussion. The medical people asserted that the calorific value of the wine was to our advantage, healthwise, in the cold of the northern Italian winter. There were the walks to be enjoyed, out of the camp, too.

In the German camp, there were no walks and no alcoholic drinks. This led to some bright sparks constructing small secret stills, in which they used the dried fruit, prunes etc., which had been allotted to them in their Red Cross parcels, from time-to-time. One such individual, would produce a small bottle of clear fluid from his pocket to lace his tea, or other innocuous beverage. In this case, the medics warned against the practice as being fraught with danger. A small number would become intoxicated and behave in a way which brought a reaction from the Germans. Actions such as climbing out of the hut windows after the lock-up. Some were attacked by the dogs on patrol and some were shot. This also applied to the foolhardy action of crossing the trip fence without permission. After hospital treatment, these miscreants were given a spell in the cooler, by the Germans. In some cases, misbehaviour was punished by being 'purged' to a *strafe lager* or punishment camp. I did not know these people very well, as we had only been in this camp a relatively short time, coming up as we had from Italy. The escapers were a much more circumspect group and the escape organisation was well on the way with three tunnels which, ironically, bore our names for the three sunken ships in Benghazi Harbour, Tom, Dick and Harry, which were used as quays for shipping there. It was the chosen one of three tunnels, Harry, which was to be finally broached from an entrance in the hut next to ours. The story of the escape has been told by a fellow Air Force PoW, from Australia, Paul Brickhill in his book, *The Great Escape.* Of the 76 who escaped through the exit hole, which was unfortunately short of the intended spot in the woods, safely over the sentry patrol path, we were notified that 43 had been shot. Another list of seven made the number of executions up to 50, allegedly on orders from Hitler himself. The list included many of the big names of the camp escape organisation.

The controller and mastermind, known as Big X, Roger Bushell, also a Squadron Leader whose name eludes me was known as Little X, but fifty years on, the names are better handled in detail in various books of the time, such as the one by Paul Brickhill, who told me after the escape that he was going to write about it and he did – marvellously.

There were occasional Air Raid warnings but fortunately, none eventuated in close proximity, although now and again we could hear what the experts in the camp declared was Berlin being bombed by the big raids. We witnessed a large American formation which we again understood, from the experts, was the big Sweinfurt ball-bearing raid. The German Air Force was intercepting the Fortresses all along their route by climbing above and diving down, picking off the victim, then continuing down out of range. From our viewpoint the slaughter was very apparent.

After Christmas 1944, we heard gunfire out to the east and by interpreting our secret radio news it had to be assumed it was the Russian advance which we had been following with a daily moving line on our 'operations room' wall map, of the whole theatre of the war. Suddenly, the word was passed around the camp by room commanders that we had to pack up what we could carry and in two hours we were to be on the road. The camp was covered in thick snow at the time so similar conditions on the roads were obviously going to make travelling along them, exceedingly difficult. In addition, over the past six months, because the Red Cross had warned that with the progress of the war, transport of our food parcels was becoming well nigh impossible. We had been existing on half rations and storing what we could against the emergency of a stoppage altogether. The Red Cross parcels were an essential supplement to the German rations scale for non-workers, as supplied to us.

There was always severe punishment by the Germans, for damage to the fabric of the camp. Now, taking the previously unheard of action, we began to pull the bunks to pieces to provide runners for sledges. With no ropes to pull them, our bedclothes had to be torn lengthwise. The resultant sledges moved beautifully on the snow and our belongings could be heaped on them. Some prisoners had been 'in the bag' for three or four years and had collected all sorts of valuable items such as professional books which were much too heavy to carry as well as food for the unknown length of our journey.

As we passed the Red Cross parcel store, we found the doors were open and a help yourself attitude prevailing. The guards would only tolerate a momentary halt, so that we could gather up some of the parcels, at 10 lb each and throw them onto our heaven-sent sledges. To lighten the loads, some were tearing at the cardboard in an effort to take the most valuable items and there was huge wastage strewn about in the snow in the dark of past midnight hours. German civilians were arriving in numbers and salvaging anything of our savings which were left behind in the floodlit area of the store.

As our long column moved along the snow-covered road, we were guarded on either side by the *Volksturm* – the peoples' army – some of whom were fierce, some just old and having greater difficulty trudging along in the snow than we young ones, even in our half-fed and weakened state. There were also the SS types shouting and raving. There's nothing quite like the Germans for shouting and raging and the language seems to suit it so well. We plodded on, pulling our Heath Robinson sledges which contained our food. Along the way we passed a line of about twenty Americans lying in the snow. They were covered in snow and looked as though they were sleeping. We were not allowed to take a closer look.

We trudged on all that night and next day with occasional brief stops for a breather and then as the second night approached, we were told we could sleep in a large adjacent stable which contained its normal occupants – the horses. By the time I squeezed in, there was only one place I could find, under a standing horse. Fortunately, it was continent!

Next morning, off we went again amid the shouting, with our sledges doing wonderful duty hauling our vital supplies and allowing us to feed ourselves on our salvaged Red Cross items, as we moved. At one point during a pause near a group at a cross-roads, we observed a good-looking German girl in riding habit, who spoke excellent English. If she was troubled by the Russians advancing, it was not visible in her deportment. Late that day, we approached the town of Muskau, feeling, in spite of the exercise, we would never be warm again. I remember I was wearing a Red Cross balaclava but the wind was blowing through the knitting and my ears threatened to drop off until I discovered two handkerchiefs which when stuffed into the balaclava stopped the wind chill on my long-suffering ears.

There was good news here, at Muskau – we were herded into a large brick circular edifice which turned out to be a glass furnace and glowing white hot. Ten minutes in there and we began to thaw out and to believe that life would go on! The steaming clothes began to dry out and frozen tins of food placed on the bricks were soon warmed and ready to eat. There was a lot of clean straw on the floor near the outer wall and soon we were sleeping our weary bodies back to normal.

At the end of a day or so of this marvellous warmth and sleeping in the straw, we learned that we would be moving on and the bad news that a thaw had set in with the snow melting rapidly. The disappearance of the snow meant we would now have to abandon our sledges and much of the heavy food, more waste and the prospect of going hungry without it. Once on the march again, we discovered another disadvantage of the thaw, blisters on the feet. Some were very lame in consequence. At long last, we reached a place called Spremburg, where we were each ladled out a mug full of minestrone-type soup which was absolutely marvellous and raised the morale of the sore-footed contingent particularly. The soup aboard, we were marched to the railway, where a line of cattle trucks awaited us and the old familiar fifty men or six horses prevailed. Luck was again on our side because it remained heavily overcast. However, we were in the trucks a long time and peeping through the ventilators we were apprehensive about attacks from Typhoons or Tempests which were prevalent at that period. On we went eventually, to the north-west, arriving at Bremen then on to a *Marlag*, or Naval PoW camp which had been evacuated and was quite empty. This necessitated a revival by us of all services – kitchen, sanitation, water and basic food supplies.

At the end of two months there, we were getting really organised and had been promised regular food parcels, a few of which had arrived, when, suddenly we were on the march again. It was now the latter part of April and the weather remained fine but to our good fortune it continued partly cloudy as we marched from Bremen to Hamburg. At Hamburg, we boarded long open army troop-carrying boats and crossed the Elb in these craft. Having been suddenly ordered out of Sagan into the deep snow, after Christmas 1944, to avoid re-capture by the Russians, it was now apparently to avoid release by the Allies, that we were being headed back by the Germans towards the East.

Once across the Elb, we were marched, under fairly clear skies, along rather back country-type roads. Marauding Tempests/ Typhoons, which were new aircraft types to most of us, were threatening us. The German guards showed them great respect by beating us to cover in the roadside ditches when threatened by them. Our seniors had devised white sheets with crude Union Jacks painted on them and these were placed on the horse-drawn four-wheeled German wagon at the rear of the column but that did not stave off attack and some of our people were killed by 'friendly fire' and others were wounded.

Along this part of the journey, the whole column would be turned into a large, usually grassed, field in the evening and we scratched together whatever food we had saved or sometimes, beet or potatoes from wayside clamps we had passed during the day. At one section of the march, a small boy fell into step alongside me on my right. I glanced down at him and saw that he was offering me an apple out of his reversed hand. He looked pleased when I thanked him. When we moved through villages, many of the houses had containers of clean drinking water outside, on the footpath. Some would offer an egg which was gratefully accepted.

Each night, in the field we had been turned into, to sleep, most of us used to make a hollow for our hip and also a mound at the head area to deflect the wind. The greatcoat from the Red Cross, was a wonderful asset as we had no bedding and no wet weather clothing. Another miracle, we had been on the road for some three weeks and during that time there had been no serious rain. This was fortunate, as we just lay down on the soil, after modification of the contours and wind deflectors aforementioned.

During the march, the security seemed to progressively lessen and it appeared possible again to escape. Our seniors advised staying with the column for safety in numbers. It had been reported that roving bunches of SS fanatics had been liquidating escapers, summarily. Everything pointed to the war coming to an end and very soon our march ended at a stable on the edge of Lübeck, where there was clean straw and it was dry and out of the wind. On reflection, we felt sorry for the farmers in whose fields, about a thousand of us had spent the night. Digging holes, building deflectors, carting stones, building little fires and generally ruining his pastures. We saw one or two who looked very distressed at the chaotic state and the clean-up job involved. The stable at Lübeck was adjacent to a little Cottage Hospital which had as its patients, some very young looking *Luftwaffe* members who were friendly and whose wounds were in need of attention. They smelt badly.

CHAPTER TEN

RELEASE AND REPATRIATION

In a day or so, two Comet tanks belonging to the 1st British Army arrived and for us we knew that for the second time, 'for us the war was over'. The tanks were quickly covered by all sorts of displaced nationals. Local German women burst into tears, others laughed and clapped and hugged and kissed the tank crews. We were told by our own seniors to stay where we were until transport arrived. Many ignored this advice/orders and started coming back with guns, food, jewellery, helmets and all sorts of souvenirs. Most eye-catching were some cars, many of which were magnificent.

We were not supposed to leave the precincts of the stables, so those of us who were still observing that order were sitting in the straw like 'Goodie, Goodie, Two Shoes', when someone said, 'Why the hell are we just sitting here, when everyone else is having a good time and enjoying the freedom?' Another came in and said, 'Look, we've a car out there, why don't you come with us into Lübeck and see what it's like?' So off we went out onto the road and got into this van – it wasn't a car – the engine started and off we went down the road. Then it stopped dead. There was a thunderous banging on the metal panelling and on the door. It turned out to be a furious Major of the Provost Corps, who ordered us out of the vehicle. He said, 'Right, if you chaps hadn't just come out of the bag this morning, you'd be going back in lock-up straight away, tonight!' So we climbed out ignominiously and went back to our straw in the stable.

The next day some British troop-carrying trucks arrived into which we climbed and sat, unseeing, until let out at what turned out to be an evacuated *Luftwaffe* Station. A sanitation truck arrived with its trained operators who lined us up to be de-loused. I don't think any of us was affected, but it was a wise precaution. The process involved applying pressure guns to us and our belongings, mainly DDT dust. In our hair, up out armpits, down our trousers, they squirted the powder everywhere. After that we had to fill in various documents before being embarked on several DC-3s which had arrived. We had a quick look round the buildings, one of which was a very grand and comfortable looking pilots' Mess – so we were told. Better than anything we had known in our time. In one of the recreation areas there was a bar and a place for 'throwing up' in, so that the person could be more fit for flying next day.

Our embarkation on to the DC3s was cancelled and we dossed down where could, on the floor, in these magnificent, but fairly bare buildings. Nothing much to eat either but we were used to scant rations and it was great to be 'free' after all the years of looking forward to it. One does get used to smaller amounts of food and we were used to coping on one meal a day, however small. When we arrived back in England, we were labelled 'suffering from Malnutrition' and issued with double ration cards! These were popular with the locals if we were invited to stay. The DC3s proved to be in wartime gear which accommodated us and all our 'rubbish'. We enjoyed just being airborne again and looking out of the small window in the side of the fuselage behind us.

After landing at Brussels we were told to stay on the airfield as we would be going on to England that day. So we stayed on the grass where we were from mid-morning until the early evening when they said, 'You'll have to get into these trucks and go to England by air in the morning! In the meantime, you'll have to be processed'. In the trucks, under the canvas tilt, we didn't see anything until we arrived at St Annes Barracks where there were more forms and of course the chaps with the DDT guns. Then we were allocated a bed and by that time it was 2300 hours. 'OK', they said, 'you are free to do what you like now. Have a look at Brussels but be sure you are on the trucks at 6.30am tomorrow to go to England'.

The war must be over we thought because we went out on the road which was brightly lit and fairly deserted. Here we were, legally free to walk down a highway. A bit further on there was one of the Army trucks with which we had recently become familiar. The crew appeared to be all female Army personnel who surrounded our little party saying they needed our help. It appeared that an Australian airman had asked for a lift and in swinging himself up into the back he had struck he head heavily on the frame of the tilt and laid himself out on the floor of the truck. I do not think we were much help, not being able to speak or read the local language and everyone in the city seemed to have gone to bed.

So much for Brussels. Anyway, the nurses dismissed us and so as it was getting on into the small hours, we found our bed spaces again at St Annes Palace. Departure time of 6.30am meant we had to be up at 6 am with just time for a shave and then into the trucks.

We were being continuously marshalled into lines and groups by our Army 'handlers' and it wasn't long before a completely new set of adjacent ex-PoWs comprised the group. Old friends were lost in the confusion, never to be seen again, in some circumstances. Anyway, we arrived back on the grass of the airfield to await our airlift which was due any minute to take us to England. Being a prisoner-of-war is good training for the waiting game and we were still waiting on the grass at midday. There was no lunch. Late afternoon we were still waiting and that, from about 7 am when we had arrived. Even we were tired of waiting with no refreshments of any sort. Then a Lancaster stopped fairly near us and we were told it would take us to England. When closer to it, the crew opened the bomb bay door on one side and we put our meagre belongings up on the other side. The door was closed and we were invited to board. We clambered up and sat on the floor, the engines still ticking over: then they roared into life and we taxied away onto the runway and the take-off.

Our arrival in England was at an airfield in the south called Wing. This time the crew opened both bomb doors and our belongings landed in a line along the runway where we gathered up what belonged to each. Next we were marshalled into line again and into the inevitable de-lousing routine, exactly as before. We emerged from this treatment getting dressed again, doing up our trousers and shrugging on our gear as we went into a hangar straight into a long line of WAAF girls who were ready to escort us to a table groaning with food. They invited us to sit down and enjoy this lovely spread and were surprised and somewhat disappointed that we were not gulping it down, and indeed that we were not raggedly attired or haggard. We had saved things to wear and carried them around so that we would be tidy for going home. This reminds me of the story of a pair of shoes I had acquired at Sagan. Young Douglas, a Scottish air-gunner, had been sent these shoes which were too big for him. I was wearing my large Red Cross army boots at the time and these shoes were a great temptation to which I had succumbed for the price of about six months Red Cross chocolate bars which came in the weekly parcels. I had to make a contract through Food Acco and sign up quite formally. This had taken place just before the Swiss Protecting Power had advised our SBO to go onto half parcels. My length of payment was automatically increased because my ration of chocolate had been halved. Meanwhile I had discovered, on the

112

circuit, that the shoes had a sole which bent in the wrong place for my feet and were painful to wear for any length of time.

When the camp had broken up and we had started the march from Sagan, I had taken the now valuable shoes, (in lost chocolate sustenance), as part of my load and I had carried them all the way to Lübeck where I eventually threw them as far as I could. I then wore my Army boots instead to go home and into the hangar at Wing.

It was now the 8th of May and it was quite dark by the time we were onto some more trucks and this time we ended our ride at an Army Camp at Great Missenden. We were met by the Army Colonel who, I remember, had one arm. He greeted us warmly and told us it was V-Day but out of regard for our arrival and our PoW status, his establishment was confined to camp, to look after us. Not the most popular decision on V-night!

We were given a meal and bedded down in tents for the night. Tired, after all day on the airfield, both days, then the reception at Wing and trucking to Great Missenden, we were more than ready for sleep. Early breakfast then trucks to the train which took us to Brighton – the Repatriation Centre – for Australia and New Zealand. We, the New Zealand RNZAF contingent, were quartered in the Grand Hotel which had been turned over to armed services occupation and management with stark furnishing and sheets of wall board covering vulnerable areas of wall etc.

Next day, we were taken along to the Metropole where a RNZAF (ex PoW) Flight Lieutenant, who had been repatriated earlier, was in charge of our kit recovery process and was running a headquarters operation to aid our repatriation. To my great surprise, my green trunk was produced. This was the trunk I had given the batman a couple of pounds to take to equipment and to ask them to forward it to Middle East. It bore labels and other evidence of having been around the Cape and possibly to Middle East, but here it was, back in Brighton. When I opened it I found it had been opened previously and one of my Service Dress Uniforms had been dry-cleaned and was ready to wear. All the Air Ministry property, such as tin hat, gas mask, gauntlets etc., had been returned to store. There was no sign of my Malta Kit although my log book was there. I was particularly sad that *all* my photographs, both personal and service ones of various targets, had been removed along with my two very good personal cameras.

We had a long briefing about a multitude of things and also how to use the services which had been laid on to help us readjust to our new-found freedom. One early detail was to see an Assistant Section

Officer Hull, on one of the upper floors. Arriving at the appointed time and room number, there was a note on the door to say she had been unavoidably called away. Later, I received another note apologising for not being there and making a further appointment, this time signed by Kathleen Hull. I went up the long stairs again to the room and there she was – a very beautiful young woman in what is known today, as a Pilot Officer's uniform. I was rather gauche, this being my first conversation for some three years or so with one of the fair sex. She was an Intelligence Officer in one of the areas of that Branch of the RAF. She asked how I had been shot down, what had happened to the aircraft and to me. Where I had been captured and what camps and so on. She seemed satisfied with my answers and having thanked me, I withdrew, quite disoriented.

The next day or so I was arraigned before the RNZAF Squadron Leader, who detailed the three options open to me but from the way it was put to me, there were, in reality, none. I could stay in the UK if I could prove I had a job to take up on my leaving the RNZAF in UK. Secondly, I could be transferred to the RAF but that was played down by the Squadron Leader as committing myself to a very long stay in a Non-Effective Pool, with still no flying. Thirdly, I could take repatriation to New Zealand where there were many flying jobs awaiting and they would be glad of my services. The officer was pressing this one and, after all, the flying was what I wanted, so I gave him that as my choice.

Several of my old Malta friends sought me out at this time. Laddie Lucas, who gave me the sad news of dear old Raoul Daddo-Langlois's demise. Porridge Kerridge, and Ian Gammidge, who gave me his sombre news about John Tucker, who he said, was one of the first off his landing craft in the Sicilian landings. Les Colquhoun wrote me a long newsy letter about how some things went after my exit and brought me up-to-date in that he was now married. Les said he took over my job, to the irritation of a Canadian flying officer, apparently.

Once these interviews and other miscellaneous duties concerned with having returned to freedom were completed, we were advised we could take leave. In this connection, we became aware of the hospitality services available in Britain and I appeared before one of the representatives who enquired about my choice of destination. Meanwhile, we were attending a daily assembly when any news of interest, (to ex-PoWs), and any special instructions were announced and detailed. It had become a ritual in my group to adjourn afterwards to a waterfront cafe for morning tea. It was while we were taking this refreshment one morning, that the attractive waitress leaned over to me and whispered that a friend of her's had asked her to ask me for a date, as she put it. She said, 'She's quite nice, a blonde'. The waitress then detailed time and place outside the cinema. I turned up as arranged and there was this tall shapely young girl standing there. I saw her several times and she took me home to her mother's apartment to meet her parent and some others of her family. She then revealed she wanted me to take her to New Zealand with me, and in those days, marriage was the only way. She was so much younger than I and nowadays, as one hears people say in a situation such as I found myself, there was no 'chemistry'. Regretfully, I thought I'd better leave it at that. I believe she became a famous skater.

The hospitality services advised me that my choices had been arranged and I was due to visit a Mrs Broad in Thames Ditton, as a beginning. The next was to be at the town of Bowness on Lake Windermere then on to Fochabers in Scotland. In association with these arrangements came names and addresses so that my rail warrants to cover these journeys could be issued and leave addresses recorded for recall if necessary, for embarkation etc.

Being invited into the warm and hospitable home of Mr and Mrs Broad was indeed a delightful experience at that time. They spared nothing in their efforts to make me as comfortable as possible and in showing me local places of beauty and interest. The resultant friendship was to last over a great many years – until the end of their lives in fact.

The ex-PoW double ration cards continued to be a feature of these travelling excursions and were most popular with my hostesses. My next arranged stay was with Mrs Harwood at Bowness on Lake Windermere. Mrs Harwood Snr, mother-in-law of my hostess, was staying in the Bowness house while Mrs Harwood Jnr awaited word of her husband, who was a prisoner-of-war of the Japanese. One of her local friends was the District Nurse, who used to have a very wide-spread practice in the Lake District. Petrol was, of course, rationed and scarce, so when they arranged for me to go on various far-flung and very interesting duty journeys, I was pleased to be thus favoured and I saw a lot of the beautiful country in the care of a wonderfully well-informed guide and driver. I also hired a boat and took my benefactors for a spin on Lake Windermere. It was mid-summer and the days seemed endless and full of enjoyment. The sight of the local squirrels cavorting about the property and the sound of the cuckoo, remain to this day.

My next hospitality stop was with Dr and Mrs Macdiarmid, at

Fochabers, in North Scotland. They met me in his Rover 12, which I thought then was the most delightful car I had been in at that time, 1945. He explained that he had become a doctor after service in the Royal Flying Corps, in World War 1, when he had been offered a University Course to qualify as a Medical Practitioner. After qualifying, he had set up practice and married, in Fochabers. Like the District Nurse in the Lake District, the doctor had sometimes to visit out of the way places in Scotland, and he chose to take me on any trip which he thought I would find interesting. One in particular, I remember, was tracing the course of the River Spey which we undertook in his Rover with the river flowing towards us as we headed south along the adjacent highway, then it slowed and finally stopped until further on it flowed south in the direction we were travelling. It was a long way up there to Fochabers, in the train, and although when I left, they hoped I would 'manage back', I never did accomplish it. Christmas cards were exchanged for many years, until a daughter wrote to say her father had died, followed, not long afterwards, by her mother.

I saw people from the Lake District a few more times, in London and in Guernsey. We had a joint trip to Jersey one day in a Dragon Rapide, (Dominie, in service terms). This was much later when Mrs Harwood's husband had been repatriated from Malaya where he had been held as a Japanese PoW. Mrs Broad became a widow, living with her son who never enjoyed robust health and they eventually decided to move from Thames Ditton to Weymouth, where her daughter lived and where I used to visit both families while I was in the RAF and where Mrs Broad's daughter, Laura, lives now, in old age herself.

Back in Brighton many of us were wondering when our repatriation would take place and in other words, when flying would start again. During the long delay, I had made some unsuccessful sorties onto the flying market. Laddie Lucas was kindness itself in suggesting ways and means. He introduced me to an older Air Commodore on the active list, who said he didn't see any difficulty, as he handed me over to a Wing Commander who took an exceedingly poor view of such an unofficial approach, which ended in a threatening attitude. BOAC said that if I had had Mosquito experience, it might have been possible but at that time they had thousands of pilots who were all in multi-engined practice, to choose from. I was out of flying practice for some three years and I had been talked out of the official RAF transfer, by the RNZAF representative.

Eventually, the embarkation notice arrived and because we were located at Brighton, we were sent on a triangle route to Blackpool to eventually board the *Andes* at Southampton! Even so, it wasn't an immediate departure from Blackpool and I remember returning in the early morning from a short visit to Glasgow, on a stormy day, which blew my SD cap off and under a lorry, beneath which I had to crawl ignominiously to retrieve it in damaged state. At Blackpool I was billeted in one of the, what seemed to be hundreds, of waterfront terrace houses which had become holiday lodgings in peacetime. All looking the same, one had to be careful to note the number or house name to be sure of entering the right one on return. Down to Southampton by train and embarkation on the *Andes* followed.

On board, the vessel was full of very noisy, time-expired aircrew types with lots of pay to spend on gambling. The ex-prisoners found it a bit overpowering and knots of us would gather at the rail and wonder if things were ever going to settle down again. Quarters were not too bad – just the noise of these types – it was a wet ship and there was often the odd drunk to cope with. We passed through the Mediterranean again but it was dark when we negotiated the central region and Malta was among the familiar sectors I had hoped to see but missed in the dark. We continued on down to Suez and after a brief stop, pressed on to Australia where the port of call was Melbourne.

As we docked, I was fairly confident that my English friends would have alerted their Melbourne ones or relatives as they had promised. I didn't know much about these kind Melbourne people but when my shipboard friends were pressing me to go ashore with them, I elected to keep watch for a message which I was fairly sure would be arriving at the Purser's office. The latter's deputies denied any knowledge of a message for me until, late in the day when everyone was returning and re-embarking, they found it! I dashed ashore to a coin phone and belatedly called the number I'd been given on the note when it was delivered. It was revealed, sadly, that these kind people had taken the day off work and been waiting adjacent to the ship – all to no avail. I could only hope that they believed that the recipient of their message had not been so remiss and not that I was just a thoughtless antipodean. There were more shocks in store. On the ship I met an officer with whom I had originally started Air Force training. I asked him what he was doing there on the ship. He told me that he had come over from New Zealand to Melbourne, in a Sunderland flying boat, to tell the Air Force repatriates that they were virtually 'all on the street', when they arrived back in their Country. I said I had been told to hurry back and that I would get a flying job. 'No,' he replied, 'you are all washed up!'

117

So, not seeing the Melbourne folk, who had been waiting for me and being hit with this disastrous news, we sailed that evening, for Wellington.

The North Island personnel on board were extremely disappointed, to put it mildly, when well out into the Tasman Sea, it was announced that as we were due in Wellington on 'Labour Day', the wharf labourers were on holiday and therefore, our first stop would be Lyttelton, the port of Christchurch. It did not affect me much but there was considerable unprintable language from the largest section of our number, which was from the North Island, as we passed through Cook Strait, who had then to wait for the ship to turn around in Lyttelton before discharging them back in Wellington.

Very little meeting of friends and relatives took place at the wharf in Lyttelton for we were bundled onto a train for the short journey through the railway tunnel, to Christchurch, where the main reunions took place.

I had been detailed to report to Wigram, where I was given my discharge and summarily transferred to the Reserve, Class A. That was that! I received notice of a gratuity of about £400 which had been credited to a special Post Office Savings Account. The interest was high, (4%), as long as it was left intact. We were told that it was to discourage inflation! There was also accrued pay to be collected covering my period of wartime service with the RAF.

CHAPTER ELEVEN

RETURN TO NEW ZEALAND

So, I was now 'out on the street', further away than ever from
flying. At that time the RNZAF had a fleet of lend lease DC-3
aircraft which were running a service up and down the Country.
This turned out to be the nucleus of National Airways Corporation
and it was possible to book a ride, free of charge for returning
personnel. I travelled to the North Island with Doug Cookson, an
old Technical School friend from Christchurch, who was an Air
Force navigator. We visited various places which we had not seen
previously. Some of them did not leave us with any enthusiasm to see
again. At Waitomo, for instance, the hotel was like an old-fashioned
railway waiting room, inhospitable-looking cold lounge with no
entertainment whatsoever such as radio or gramophone and no
books. Next day we were taken on a rowing boat trip through
the caves by a guide who was unable to tell us much at all. We
did enjoy a successful trout fishing excursion on Lake Taupo and
delivered several large fish to the hotel kitchen. We were served a
minute portion of one, at breakfast next morning.

Back in the South Island I ran into another original course friend
and he told me he had been to see a Wing Commander in Wellington
RNZAF HQ about this business of being thrown on the street with no
chance of ever touching an aircraft again. It seemed he had been
granted a short familiarisation course and I thought I would give it
a go as well. I managed to book a seat on a Wellington bound DC-3
again – they used to land and take off from Paraparaumu in those
days. Once in the City, I made my way to RNZAF HQ to beard the lion
in his den. I explained to a Wing Commander Gamble that I hadn't
flown since being shot down in 1942 and would greatly appreciate
some flying before finally being grounded. He was not too keen at
first, but after some thought and questions, he gave me ten days at
Wigram Central Flying School to get whatever flying I could manage
in that time. I was delighted.

Reporting to CFS, I discovered a Flight Lieutenant 'Mick' R.K.

Walker was officer commanding and he delegated a Flight Lieutenant Eccersall to be my instructor, after I had enjoyed a passenger flight in an Oxford for an hour. Next day, we climbed into a DH82 Tiger Moth for some circuits and landings. Another day, I did one hour and ten minutes' solo in the Tiger, polishing up the circuits and landings after being three years earthbound. After the third day, we switched to a Harvard III, where after some 'circuit bashing' we practised some aerobatics and spinning. On my penultimate day, I was awarded an hour's dual in the Oxford and on the final day, day ten, an hour ten minutes solo in the Harvard. That was my lot, 16 hours 40 minutes. It did allow me to go to my old Canterbury Aero Club now located at Harewood, where after a 15 minute check, I was away, solo, on the Tiger. A friend of the old club days, 'Norm' Suttie, who was now flying for Air Travel Ltd on the West Coast, offered me the opportunity to fly a Tiger for him to Hokitika. I was pleased to have this chance and I took a met. office passenger, J. Kirby, through the Otira Gorge. I had, incidentally, meanwhile, resurrected my 'A' Licence and I applied for and gained a 'B' licence, which entitled me to fly commercially. Nevertheless, I was inexorably on the street and looking for a job. There were plenty of 'no future' jobs on offer, but it looked as though flying was out for the time and although the successor to my old employer invited me back I had always wanted a change. At one time I was generously offered an adult apprenticeship which had some appeal. I went along to the much lauded Rehabilition Centre. They claimed to 'lead the world', but I was turned down flat! 'You go back to the job you had before the war.'

It was about this time, after I had informed my sponsors, Ritchie and Sherrard, of the Rehab. decision, I noticed the Meteorological Office was recruiting observers. I had done the Meteorological Course at *Luft* 3 and the 2nd class Navigators' Syllabus so I applied and was accepted. This meant attending a live-in course in Blenheim at Woodbourne Aerodrome, an Air Force Station, where we were allocated clean and comfortable barrack accommodation in what had previously been a flying school. It was a four weeks' course with a uniformed RNZAF Warrant Officer as the Chief Meteorological Instructor. During the course, there were a lot like me, former pilots, and we were looking for gems of any sort in the situations vacant columns of the dailies.

One of these course members, David Morgan, saw that Pan American Airline, was looking for freight handlers and as the wages were better than we would get, initially, in the Met. Office, he and another chap applied for and got a job with Pan American in Auckland. He,

David, before he retired and the company ceased operating in this country, eventually became the Director of Pan American in New Zealand. After the Course there was an examination on all we had learned about cloud recognition, fronts, air masses, winds and temperatures. Other practical subjects like plotting weather maps, reading meteorological instruments, i.e. thermometers, barometer, (mercury), rain gauges, balloon wind directions and speed-finding day and night, by using a theodolite were practised and learned.

After the Course, I was posted to Wigram at about the same time as one of the young forecasters, Clive Allpress. Being a forecaster, he was entitled to live in the Officers' Mess accommodation. He generously elected to join me in the Sergeants' Mess where we had many good daily games of tennis, billiards, snooker and table tennis. He was very good at all those small ball games. Our chief forecaster was a gentleman by the name of Jim Hunter and we were a very happy office on the top of the control tower. My duties were allocated by a Ken Brown who had been a Sergeant in the Met. Office in war time and had carried on as a civilian. Ken made out the duty roster. While he came in for a normal day shift, the rest of us, observers, did a seven and a half hour shift for four days then two off, except after night duty when we had an extra sleeping day.

Our observation duties were of two-hourly rotations reading the various instruments and recording these readings in the book for the record and climatology etc and sending off balloons and recording their path through the air by means of a theodolite. At night, we used a lantern on the tail of the balloons made from cardboard and cellophane with a lighted candle in the middle. Inflating the balloons with hydrogen and launching them in a strong wind at night required care and skill to succeed. Weather reports had to be despatched on the teleprinter and other places further south had to have theirs switched through to Wellington. Plotting weather maps with the international weather symbols of the time, was quite time consuming and they had to be ready for the forecaster at the times laid down. In the morning after night duty, the weather map had to be completely plotted before the duty forecaster came on at 7 o'clock. The hourly reports were a continuing hourly responsibility all day and night.

It was while I was reflecting on what I would do with my now, post-war life, that the RAF advertised for experienced pilots to return to the UK to take up Extended Service Commissions. Naturally, I applied for one of those and whilst it was a long time before I had anything other than an acknowledgement, in due course I was notified I would go before a touring RAF selection board which would be in New Zealand to assess and choose applicants.

During my time at *Luft* 3, Sagan, one day when I was walking around the 'circuit' I met an old school classmate, Jerry Taylor. He was strolling with a Squadron Leader Trent, who had been leading the Squadron when Jerry was shot down. Jerry introduced me to Squadron Leader Trent which turned out to be a happy coincidence because when the Selection board arrived in New Zealand, chaired by an RAF Wing Commander, Squadron Leader Trent – now decorated with the Victoria Cross, was his deputy. My Met. office contemporaries and the chief forecaster, Jim Hunter, all wished me luck as the appointed time for my interview came around. The interview room was in the same building as the Met. office on the ground floor, while we were located on the top floor.

The interview was pleasant and it helped having met Squadron Leader Trent previously, but the result had to be notified from London. I was to discover, by notification, much later, that I had been successful. I was appointed to an Extended Service Commission in the rank of Flight Lieutenant.

Meanwhile, life went on as usual and then I received a letter from the RNZAF, asking me whether I would like to go to Japan as a member of the Army of Occupation, flying Corsairs. I had not heard positively, from the RAF at this time but as I had been let down so badly, previously, by the RNZAF I decided to turn this offer down and await my fate with the RAF application. Eventually, my acceptance for the RAF Extended Service Commission of four years in the rank of Flight Lieutenant, came through and I was able to notify the Met. Office of my plans. These plans included a berth on the *Brisbane Star*, sailing from Port Chalmers. The *Brisbane Star* was, of course, the convoy ship in Valletta Harbour where Warburton had detailed me to take his girl friend Christine, to lunch, back in those tumultuous days in Malta, 1942. The *Brisbane Star* in the August '42 convoy had been torpedoed on the bow which released its anchor chains and so slowed it right down while putting great strain on the forward bulkhead. Captain Riley, notwithstanding, had turned his vessel around and reversed until he was able to shore up the bulkhead and also relieve the ship of the trailing anchor chains. Eventually, the *Brisbane Star* was able to rejoin the other three merchant vessels, the survivors of twelve merchant ships which had been successful in making it to Malta and finally, the tanker *Ohio* had made it to Valletta too. Numerous warships in that convoy had been lost as well.

CHAPTER TWELVE

THE ROYAL AIR FORCE AND FLYING AGAIN

When I saw the *Brisbane Star* again some five years later, in Port Chalmers, it had meanwhile, been to Buenos Aires, where the severely damaged bow had been filled with concrete which gave it a bulbous effect, not unlike some of the modern freighters but in a more crude form.

Captain Riley was greeting the fifteen or so passengers and I found I was allocated a seat at the Captain's table. I brought up the subject of the missed lunch. He said he had waited hours and hadn't been too pleased. Anyway, that soon passed and we were frequently reminiscing in his flat on the Bridge as we traversed the wide Pacific to the Panama Canal. The new day often had dawned before I was released to my cabin and sleep following generous portions of the good Captain's Johnnie Walker. There were various RAF people on board who, like me, had been accepted on an extended engagement in the UK. There were also other passengers travelling to the UK including a lady doctor who revealed she was travelling free, as the ship's doctor. I was again put in charge of the air force draft. There was a Squadron Leader passenger who was returning to the RAF from leave in New Zealand. He was obviously one who had not accepted RNZAF promises and had stayed on in the RAF to get on with a career in flying, which was to his liking.

We refuelled at Curacao and then on across the Atlantic to finally dock at Tilbury. From Tilbury, I was despatched by RAF movements, to 5 PDC at Liverpool. I was hardly in the door of that unit before I was being asked for my leave address to be put on my leave documents with Rail Warrants attached. I could only think of the Broad family in Thames Ditton so when I got in touch with them, I was warmly welcomed to stay. After an indefinite time on leave, probably two months, I was eventually posted as a supernumerary officer to Thorney Island on the south coast not far from Havant and on the Solent. As an extra to establishment, I found I was in line for all various committees of adjustment, of surveys of various kinds, sorting redundant documents and of course Station Duty Officer.

Soon after I arrived, I met another NZ officer, Ian Burgess who had fortunately found a niche for himself in Air Traffic Control. He was, however, like me, a supernumerary, so he joined me on some committee work and Station duties. Thorney Island was the home of the 'Survival and Rescue Training Course', and so Ian Burgess and I were both able, at different times, to attend this course with permission from the Station Headquarters. The more enjoyable aspects were taking the airborne lifeboats across the Solent to the Isle of Wight. I was in the party on two occasions. The first time we stopped at Ryde for a marvellous lunch. On this first exercise the instructor had emphasised the necessity to switch off the Austin marine motor early, as these boats had no neutral or reverse gear. On arrival, we heard a loud cracking and some strident remarks and when we looked over we saw the instructor's team going under the pier and being dismasted in the process. Our crew had a Lieutenant Commander RN on board who was also doing the course, so we felt fairly confident that we were in the right company – and so it turned out. The second trip, this time to Shanklin, was even more enjoyable with lobster lunch etc. At Thorney Island there were also all sorts of aircraft from Lancasters down to Mosquitoes, Meteors and Spitfires. I was looking enviously at the pilots who were flying these aircraft.

The President of the Mess Committee (PMC) was a Squadron Leader who used to terrorise most of the junior officers and one day one Naval officer said something which didn't please the PMC who responded with an uppercut which laid him out cold. The bar, where this took place, cleared as if by magic, leaving the PMC with a few of his own flight and the unfortunate Naval officer, on the floor.

The officer in charge of the Marine section at Thorney Island, having the name Funnel, was certain to acquire the nickname of 'Smokey'. On the Survival and Rescue Course, in a semiofficial capacity, we all learned everything about the emergency radio on the airborne lifeboat and how to energise it with its handle. We also learned about the manipulation of the rigging and the erection of the mast. There was an underfloor Austin marine motor to propel the boat as well as a sail. There were rockets to fire lifelines, in various directions all round the boat and these were fired semi-automatically when the boat was level, after having descended from the aircraft, on its parachutes. Rations and a waterproof book of directions or instructions were included in the thoughtful design of the boat.

While enjoying the course, we were told that Station Headquarters had agreed to our attendance on condition that should we be required to perform any Station duty, we would have to give up the course and because we were not on it officially, it would not be entered on our documents. Flight Lieutenant Bill Bedford was a course member, who was from RAF Finningley, where he was a Pilots' Refresher Course Instructor. One day when we were discussing the Pilots' Refresher Course, he asked me if I would like him to be my instructor at Finningley when my course posting eventually came through. I jumped at the chance and he was true to his word when I arrived there.

Once again I was flying on a singles course on the Harvards and Spitfire 16s. The latter, being virtually a refined Spitfire Mark 9 with the Packard Merlin engine and hence all American threads and fittings. On the course we were meant to qualify for an Instrument Rating, White or Green, which had become a requirement, post war. Consequently, we were logging actual cloud flying, whenever possible. Bill Bedford being something of a genius in this direction would do some aerobatics in cloud then when the gyros had toppled, would hand over. I would have to sort the situation out under his direction on primaries, i.e. without gyro instruments. Sometime later, Bill Bedford became involved at an early stage in the 'Harrier' development and was the star performer at Farnborough and similar venues throughout the world. A wonderful instructor and an exceptional pilot. I have always felt privileged to have been his pupil.

After the Refresher Course at Finningley, I was posted to RAF Leuchars, in Fife, Scotland, where was situated the Photographic Reconnaissance Operational Training Unit. My operational flying career had been almost exclusively on Spitfires, starting with fighters Marks 1 & 2, PR 4, Fighter 5 and the Mark 16 at Finningley. I had had extensive operational war experience on Spitfire Photo Reconnaissance but now I learned my fate was to be taught the PR 'trade' at this OTU staffed by instructors who were not experienced in Photographic Reconnaissance. All this was a great disappointment to be instructed apparently by inexperienced instructors in matters of which I was already familiar. The course was a very small one – by numbers – there being one Mosquito crew of Flight Lieutenant Turner and Sergeant Maurice Huggett and the Spitfire pilot, myself. I think there were three flying instructors, a navigation instructor and various others who gave lectures on disparate subjects like meteorology, engines and airframes etc., all of which we had covered numerous times in our careers and also, recently, in the

Refresher mode. I wondered how all those instructors managed to fill in their time. Unfortunately, I contracted a stubborn cold during the course and this, naturally, interfered with my high altitude flying programme. As a result, I was sent off for X-rays to a combined Maternity and TB Hospital situated along the Forth River. While visiting that establishment I was left for hours to cool my heels in a room with tables full of open case-files of the most gruesome kind. The result of this visit to this hospital was explained to me while I was there, by a doctor of Polish extraction, who said my X-rays showed early development of Bronchiectasis. When I suggested I stop smoking, he said he didn't think it would make any difference. I did, however, give up smoking and I was able to continue and complete my flying programme. I mentioned the Polish doctor's diagnosis to a later Medical Board who said he must have been joking. No one has been able, since, to find any trace of the Pole's diagnosed condition.

While the three of us were on this course of nice to be flying but not learning anything new, there was the Station 'At Home' on Battle of Britain Day. The Spitfire 'Instructor' was billed to give a display and he declared he would 'show' the Meteors, who would be visiting, a thing or two. He did! While passing in front of the large crowd which included his pregnant fiancé, he approached at very high speed in a dive and appeared to start a barrel roll. There was a loud crack and the port wing folded and a large piece of cowling fell off, fortunately missing the crowd. The main part of the aircraft continued with its momentum around behind some buildings where the sickening crump and column of black smoke spelled the tragic end to the day. The Air Ministry investigator showed me the wing spar where it had been torn apart with the 'excessive stick force.'

My course finished and Turner, Huggett and myself, who had become firm friends meanwhile, were now posted to RAF Benson, of familiar times in 1942, when I had been given Spitfire AB300 and told to fly it to the Middle East, just like that. I was now posted to No.541 Squadron, commanded by Squadron Leader Verity, DSO, DFC, equipped with Spitfire PR Mark XIX. We were engaged in a variety of standing order tasks such as Town and Country planning, some spot targets as they arose and continuation training, such as flying up the east coast of England to Scotland and back at 400 feet taking oblique photographic shots of specific targets. This was a most enjoyable exercise especially in good weather. Other tasks and exercises were carried out at thirty to forty thousand feet. The Group Headquarters, which controlled Benson, was located up a gentle hill adjacent to the Station and within walking distance. I had expressed my desire for a broadening of my experience to my CO Squadron Leader Verity, who agreed that I should approach the Group P2, (officers' posting), about a PR Mosquito conversion course. The first time I approached the P2 officer, (a Squadron Leader), he said he could not do anything about my request at that moment but perhaps he could if I saw him again, in about a fortnight's time. This trudging up the hill combined with a long wait outside his office and the come back in a fortnight or so went on for some months without the slightest advance being made in my quest for the Mosquito conversion. I don't think the officer had any intention of exerting himself on my behalf and I think he had banked on my tiring early of the effort. Finally, he said, 'I don't think there is any point in you coming up here. You are wasting my time and yours.' I didn't tire of the idea, but one day after that, Squadron Leader Verity and I were in the bar at Benson when we were joined by Wing Commander S.O. Bufton, CB, DFC, the Benson OC Flying, who greeted us, and after the usual pleasantries, addressed Sqn Ldr Verity with, 'I don't suppose you know of a Flight Lieutenant Mosquito pilot spare do you?' Sqn Ldr Verity looked at me and said to the Wg Cdr 'Old Harry here is keen – what about him?' The Wgt Cdr looked at me quizzically and said, 'Is that so?' To my positive reply he said 'We'll soon fix that!' Within the week, I was on my way to RAF Driffield, in Yorkshire to attend a Mosquito Conversion Course.

We were a mixed bag of characters on the course. Some of our number had been on Mosquitoes previously and one such, Mirro Mansfeld, a Czech didn't lose any time in practising his aerobatics in the Mosquito and sometimes on one engine. After we went solo in the Mark III Mosquito and had some local practice, we were sent off with a Navigator in the Mark VI Mosquitoes to practise cross-country navigation exercises. This was a new experience to have a navigator with a Gee box to help navigation – if it worked and the navigator could use it. Unfortunately the navigator I drew was a bit of a broken reed and he was often losing us and appealing to me to find us again. One of our best trips together was at 25,000 feet from Driffield down to Romney on the south coast area at night.

As we passed London, it was an unforgettable sight for us. It was as if a large collection of sparkling beautiful jewels were laid out on a black velvet cloth. Other air traffic was fairly scarce at night, in those days and we were surprised when, on return, we were asked if we had seen anything of Hensby, another Course pilot. He had left earlier than we had. We did not see Hensby and his navigator again. It appeared he had suffered something like oxygen starvation and had dived into the Romney Marshes with his navigator and his machine.

Another unusual incident at this time was of a Mosquito VI, which called 'downwind' in the circuit at night and didn't land or call again. 'Downwind' with undercarriage down at that time should have been followed by 'finals' as he turned on final approach to land but there was nothing further. The night was spent advancing the possibilities of a landing elsewhere and so on. Next morning, a farmer reported he had found the Mosquito on his land behind a hedge with the tail showing above it. The aircraft had run along the ground and into a very strong wire fence which had demolished the cockpit and its two occupants. The aircraft altimeter had been set one thousand feet high. In other words, when he began his downwind leg with altimeter reading say, 1200 feet he would actually have been at 200 feet.

While at Driffield, we had to take part in an escape and evasion exercise where we were dropped in the countryside and had to find our way back without being caught by the police – and they were out in force. It was very cold and frosty and we were crawling about on the frost-covered soil. My navigator was not much help. He did not seem to have much idea of what was required in the way of stealth. Eventually he stood up at an inappropriate moment, when we were pounced on literally by all these police who were everywhere and had been stalking us. As they sat on us on the crisp frosty ground, I shouted, loudly, 'Hi, you're killing me, get off!' So they got off and with that, I ran away as hard as I could go. They eventually caught me again and this time they held me fast. We were both taken back to the local police lock up where the officer in charge suggested it would be a black mark on our records for allowing ourselves to be caught. Being in the police cell was quite interesting really – so very different from being a prisoner-of-war. Early next morning some RAF transport arrived to take us back to Driffield.

At the end of the Driffield Mosquito Course, I was posted back to Benson only this time, to 540 Squadron on the Mosquito PR34. Wonderful! Number 540 Squadron was now a one flight Squadron, commanded by Squadron Leader Chilton. The duties were Photo Reconnaissance again but with a navigator to guide progress on photographic runs from the bomb-aiming position. Much more accurate runs could be made for mapping purposes and all the other advantages which accrue from having the company and two pairs of eyes on the job.

There were numerous long distance sorties and one which was

memorable, was across the North Sea from Leuchars to Norway and Russia. The Norwegians had requested photographs of their country in the vicinity of their Russian border. The Norwegians were most anxious to ensure that we did not cross the border in case the Russians shot us down which they probably would have done at that time in the Cold War. After all they eventually shot down a Korean Boeing 747 full of passengers.

Jerry Dolezeal, my navigator for this sortie, and I carried out our task across Norway and the photography involved, to our satisfaction and then set course for home from the Norwegian west coast. We were flying at about 30,000 feet so after clearing the land I reduced height to 25,000 feet over the sea, at which time, by manipulating our oxygen masks we were able to eat the snack sandwiches we had brought with us. About mid way across the North Sea a red warning light relating to the starboard engine, started to shine. There was no other indication of a malfunction. Everything was so normal it was decided it must be an electrical fault in the warning system so we carried on to base with the warning red light on, and the engine performing perfectly in all respects.

Another long distance sortie was scheduled to be from Benson to a point along the south-east coast of France where we were to land at Istres. Approaching Istres however, their control on account of the weather declined permission to join and land so I continued flying to land at Gibraltar. This was the first time I had been back to Gibraltar since my pioneering trip from Portreath in AB300 in March 1942. All the feverish runway building activity had been completed long since and a long wide landing path greeted our approach. Before leaving Benson on what had turned out to be a five hour flight because of the sandstorm prohibiting our landing at Istres, we had been informed that one of our Squadron was unserviceable at Gibraltar after a collision with a large bird, probably a seagull. Sure enough, the crew were keen to show us where the bird had lodged in one of their leading edge radiators. Our CO seemed anxious to have confirmation of the damage, whereupon he requested that I hand over the Mosquito I had been flying and await the repair of the damaged one to fly it back to Benson. At Gibraltar, the repair job was obviously not getting any priority, so after some two weeks wait, I requested a return by some other means. This request was granted and I was given a lift on a Halifax flight destined for Aldergrove, in Northern Ireland. Finding somewhere to sit, for what turned out to be a nine-hour journey, was not easy in a very dirty aircraft. My best uniform was covered in grease and oil etc., when I finally returned

to Benson on 23 April 1949, following a night's enforced stay at RAF
Aldergrove.

Flying continued apace and I had become the Flight Commander,
in this one flight squadron. There were some more very interesting
assignments and one of these was designated Hush Hush where we
had to fly up and down the mainland of the British Isles 30,000
feet for what turned out to be for five hours. Before take-off a
funnel-shaped filter had been fitted to the top of the aircraft cabin.
On return, the flight sergeant climbed up to remove it. Climbing
down, he placed the object in a polished wooden box which had
been offered by a well-dressed civilian woman who had arrived in
a black chauffeur-driven saloon car.

My navigator and I were not proffered any specific explanation
at the time but after an interval, it was revealed that the Russians
indeed had exploded a nuclear bomb and our trip of long duration
had confirmed what at the time, had been suspected before our flight
up and down the British mainland

My flying activity at Benson was interrupted by a mysterious
virus-type infection. My blood count and other clinical indicators
were awry and it was several weeks before I was able to continue
enjoying the Mosquito again. I was confined to station sick quarters
for some time followed by light station duties until I was able to
begin flying again. My pleasure and satisfaction of the flying and
Squadron life was terminated one day by the Squadron Adjutant
announcing that I had been posted to the Central Flying School,
Flying Instructors' Course at Little Rissington with preliminary at
Brize Norton. I protested and enquired about having the posting
cancelled only to be told that as it was an Air Ministry posting,
I would have to go. I was reminded that while I was trailing up
and down to the Group HQ requesting a transfer to the Mosquito
Squadron and being told I was wasting my time and the P2 Officer's
as well, that a request came in for volunteers to go to Central Flying
School and I had forgotten I'd said 'Yes, I'll go,' in desperation. I
could have wept. It was months ago and it had completely slipped
my mind in the joy of my Mosquito career in the making!

So off I went to Brize Norton after saying goodbye to my Squadron
and friends on 540 PR Mosquito Squadron. At Brize Norton, Course
No 113, of which I was now a member, were welcomed, photographed
and initiated into what the requirements of the six months' Course to
follow, would be.

After a month of basic Harvard practice, we transferred, as a unit,
to Little Rissington, for the remaining five months. There we were able

to fly various types of aircraft such as the Baliol, Spitfire, Mosquito, Meteor and the Lancaster. The latter mainly for experience but I qualified on all the others.

At Central Flying School, Little Rissington, we were again required to qualify for an instrument rating which was a fairly new ticket although I had obtained one at Finningley. I had to confirm my new rating on a green card which was the higher rating of the time. In order to obtain the number of instrument hours, we were detailed to fly mutual exercises in the Harvard. This meant half the sortie was in the front cockpit, as safety pilot. Then we had to land and change over to the back cockpit, under the hood. There were several officers of other nationalities on the course and most of them were quite compatible. However, there were two Iraqis, a Major and a Lieutenant with whom, apart from some difficulty with the language, most of us felt fairly insecure whilst under the hood with one of these chaps acting as safety pilot in the front. They said nothing even when, judging by the turbulence, we appeared to have passed through the slipstream of another aircraft. When the exercise time was up, it was necessary to come out from under the hood and find the way back to base because the Iraqi safety pilot relied on the back seat student for everything. It was hopeless to address a question to this pair.

After completing the CFS Course, I graduated as B-1 category Instructor and I was posted to No. 3 Flying Training School at RAF Feltwell in East Anglia, with several others from the Course. At Feltwell, The FTS was equipped with Percival Prentices in the *ab initio* squadrons and Harvards in the 'Wings' course squadrons. There were three hangars regarded as the 'flights' with the fourth devoted to maintenance. One hangar of the flying Wing was exclusively occupied by the Prentice Squadron and two hangars allocated to the four Harvard flights, – A & B in one, C & D in the second, E & F in the third. I was posted to 'F' flight which was on the extreme end of the last hangar in the row. The Flight Commander in the post when I arrived, was in the process of departing and his post was taken up by Flight Lieutenant 'Jake' Jacobs, who quickly set about overhauling the flight organisation to conform to his penchant for orderly systems. It was not long, however, before he saw a posting to the Lebanon which he wanted and he was successful in his application to go there. I was appointed Flight Commander in his place with powers of Subordinate Commander. I was now responsible for a Course of some thirty pupils, an inventory of eight aircraft and a staff of ten flying instructors. The ground crew disciplinary matters were my responsibility also.

It was about this time that Yvonne, a friend of mine from New Zealand, had made her way to the UK with a companion and having been advised of their imminent arrival, I met them at Waterloo Station, in my Vauxhall 10 car which I had bought in Cheltenham while at CFS, and I transported them to their accommodation in London before returning to Feltwell.

At Feltwell, I occupied a very active instructional posting, running a busy flying programme which I made up in detail, daily for the following day. There were various permutations of pupils' syllabus, leave schedules as well as absences because of sickness etc. In order to keep my own instructional category intact, it was necessary to have several pupils of my own. In order to take over as Flight Commander I had had to work hard to obtain the A2 Instructor Category essential and in addition, the CFS 'Examining Wing' visited from time to time when they would carry out continuation training and ground checks to ensure a high standard was being maintained by all flying personnel. This was also checked by the pupil pilots' progress records and efficiency. The pupils' 'record of training' books which I had to examine and remark upon, at least once a month, in writing. Night flying brought an even more hectic time. The programme had to have even more permutations applied, of hours flying, number of flights, number of solo hours, before check, cross-country exercises and so on. After finishing a night of flying, it was necessary for me to co-ordinate what had been achieved that night with a schedule for the next night and in order to get it published, (typed), and distributed to the engineering and messing staffs, pilots and Flying Wing, I had to push it under the Flying Wing Adjutant's door before I could get my head on the pillow. It was usually broad daylight before I could close my eyes in slumber. Imagine my chagrin when, the following afternoon, I woke and discovered the F/W Adjutant had still to action that night's programme I had lost sleep over the previous night! Mine was a full-time job at Feltwell but I was on top of it and looking back, it was probably the most productive time of my life.

The training day was divided up into morning and afternoon schedules which seemed to be universal at the time. One half of the course flying in the morning and changing over at midday, after lunch. One day the Wing Commander Flying arrived in my office to say he had allocated two supernumerary Squadron Leaders to me as supernumeraries in F Flight, to be initiated into running a flight and flying instruction generally, before they took over the flying training squadrons, for which they had been assigned. Both of these officers had passed out from their CFS Course with the lower B2 category and the Wing Commander Flying hoped I would help them both to gain B1 and eventually A2. One in one half of the course, the other one in the other half.

One of these two was Squadron Leader Len Trent, VC – the same Len Trent I had met previously, once with my chum Jerry Taylor at Sagan, and again as a member of the RAF selection board in New Zealand. He was now married with a small postwar son and somewhere else, a prewar daughter. After my current Squadron Commander, Squadron Leader Jennings, moved on, Len assumed the former's mid-hangar office and virtual command of the No. 3 Training Squadron. He would now monitor my official correspondence and generally 'oversee' the operation of the two Harvard flights in the Hangar of which mine was one. He was obviously being groomed for 'stardom' with his VC and so he was often absent on courses and visits of one sort or another. When on the Station at weekends, some of us would motor up to the north coast of Norfolk – to Cromer or another of the watering places within easy reach. On these occasions, Len would opt to travel in my Vauxhall 10 instead of in his own Y Model Ford 8, which was something of a puddle-jumper, with his wife and small son. He had been a low handicap golfer in his day and at his suggestion, on Wednesdays, sports afternoons, we would adjourn to our deserted satellite, Methwold, for a hit around the grassed areas.

Battle of Britain day, in September, always prompted a special display of some sort and my predecessor, Jake Jacobs during his time as OC 'F' Flight, designed a really good one involving a staged train with bombing and explosions in a set piece which everybody thought was excellent entertainment. The year of 1952 came along and somehow it was decided that our new Queen should be honoured by us formating E.R. with Harvards in the sky. Len Trent, VC was nominated to be at the head of this display but just as it was about to be organised, he was called away. 'OK Harry, it's over to you now', he said with a chuckle, as he departed. From memory the formation involved twenty Harvards and the practice for this event had to take place after the normal flying schedule day. Forming up the two letters was not too bad but turning the whole formation and arriving at the airfield on precise time, was much more difficult.

Getting near the day in mid-September, Len's charming wife, Ursula, generously extended an invitation to my now fiancée Yvonne, to stay overnight with them to witness the B of B display, which Yvonne graciously accepted. On the day, Len Trent had obtained leave from whatever he was doing, away from the Station and I left him and

Yvonne in my comfortable office, overlooking the airfield, to await the 'ER' in the sky, whilst I set off with my unwieldy formation.

In the event it went off quite well, from my position up front, we seemed to be in good form and we arrived dead on time and the stream landing afterwards went off very well indeed. At the parking area I leapt out of my aircraft and dashed in to my office to receive the verdict from my Squadron Commander and my fiancée. They looked a little ill at ease and no wonder! While my big moment was being enacted they were inside a visiting Wellington aircraft with the engines running. They had not seen or heard a thing!

Postings usually lasted about two years and contemporaries of mine were moving on about that timespan to other postings so I began to take an interest in other flying jobs on offer which were to my liking, as they were canvassed. I had been at Feltwell for over two years. After three years I was still being met with a kindly refusal to let me go and an assurance, after my long service at Feltwell, that I would be placed in a posting type of my choice. I was keen to continue my multi-engine experience, an appetite whetted by the Mosquito that was my preference. My only real posting aversion was to Northern Ireland where 'difficult' and 'bad boy' personnel seemed to be shunted and anyway, it was more of the same – Harvards etc. After three and a half years at Feltwell, Yvonne and I had arranged to be married and we had organised a shoestring Registry Office ceremony, down in London. One of my instructors, Phil Cox, was a volunteer best man and Yvonne co-opted Elizabeth Armstrong as bridesmaid. My new Squadron Commander of the time, Squadron Leader Dyson, came to see me, with a worried look, to say that the newish (South African) Station Commander and a Group Captain had vetoed my Squadron Leader's collection for a wedding present, because I had not invited the whole station to my wedding. No, it was not a joke! I was surprised at the Group Captain's decision and especially as I have already mentioned, the South African PoW's in Italy had shown great humanity and gone out of their way with help in the giving of clothing and other spare items, when I possessed only what I stood up in at that time.

The Group Captain attended an Officers' Mess meeting shortly after the wedding present veto, during which he proposed another officer's present would be the subject of a collection. He stood up and made an emphatic appeal for contributions as he wanted this officer to receive something worthwhile, from his fellow officers. The point about this is that although this officer's wedding was not, at the time, far off, I did not see any general invitation to the Station or, in fact, any invitation to his wedding. In the event, 'F' Flight arranged a secret collection and surreptitiously gave me an engraved table cigarette lighter. In the circumstances, I have treasured, over the years, this little gift from the officers and men of 'F' Flight. At about this time too, being winter, there were long interruptions to the flying programmes and directly after my marriage, I was detailed to spend the next two weekends on camp, awaiting a change in the weather. Yvonne was at our rented flat in Kingston, London, meanwhile. Negotiations were underway, by me, to buy a large caravan, to be sited at the adjacent but un-manned airfield at Methwold, where it was possible to use mains power and water and there were many station personnel living in these vans. Other accommodation simply did not exist. Fortunately, the last paper and signature for the caravan purchase had not been completed when the Wing Commander Flying came, literally, running into my office on the corner of the end hangar saying he had come along himself to say I had been posted. This, because I was, so he said, the only time-expired category A2 instructor in the entire Training Command. He was there, in person, he said, to break to me that he was afraid that my posting was to be to a new Flying Training School at Cluntoe in Northern Ireland. He said he was unable to stop it. I could not help wondering whether my posting had anything to do with the Group Captain's earlier attitude.

At Feltwell, at mid term and at the end of the pupils' course when they would qualify for the flying badge, (wings), I used to invite other senior flying personnel to act as flying examiners. It was established practice at Feltwell. Mostly this went off quite well and was endorsed by all as a good idea. There was one exception; one of those invited. There was one Squadron Leader who my instructors pleaded with me not to invite as he would usually tie up a pupil and an aeroplane for a whole half day and then, quite possibly, would want to examine the pupil again on another day. I knew their criticism to be valid, but there were pressures on me to use this officer. I endeavoured to use him as little as I could afford to. Unfortunately, I learned he was now to be my senior in running a Headquarters Flight/Squadron. I felt sick at heart. There were all those promises too, that I would be going back to Mosquitoes or on to Canberras. At Cluntoe, it would be more of the same – Harvards.

I collected Yvonne from London and packed our meagre belongings in the Vauxhall, to motor to the Irish ferry. We heard that on the previous voyage to the one we were about to take, that the ship had been 'pooped' and sunk in the Irish Sea, with loss of life. Our journey, thankfully, was uneventful and after unloading the car, I dropped Yvonne off at an hotel in Cookstown, while I reported to the newly-restored, ex-vandalised, Station of RAF Cluntoe, No. 2 Flying Training School – Harvards. I was appointed OC Headquarters Flight, whilst the Squadron Leader, was OC HQ Squadron.

It seemed that while I was at Feltwell for the three and a half years, all my time was spent on the job. If I was not flying, I was administering it. I held three inventories which had various little duties adhering. I had been internally posted to the Cadets' Mess to live. That involved off-duty supervisory duties. At this time in the Cold War, there were various station defence schemes which also involved living-in personnel, at weekends. All in all there was little personal free time. Now at Cluntoe, I was a married officer and I found I was relatively free to study for the extra subjects of the promotion examination and it behove me to get on with this since I had been appointed to a permanent commission. The opportunity now arose to attend the Officers' Administration Training School Course at Bircham Newton, in England, which I grasped with alacrity. I sat the promotion examination later that year and, as a result, passed. Meanwhile, I had found a small terrace house in a little Londonderry town called Moneymore, which had been standing empty, some said, for a decade. Anyway, the owners accepted my application to rent it and we moved in to clean up the accumulation of dust. The two up and two down, rooms were small and we used to say you had to back out of them to turn round. The idea of coping with a solid fuel range and a limited water supply seem enjoyably distant now although we did manage quite well. We even adopted a little Fox Terrier dog in Magherafelt and handed over some five pounds to the outstretched Irish hand belonging to the man who arranged the deal.

My new Australian Squadron Leader, CO had married a WAAF officer in England and they were expecting their first child. He, like Len Trent, preferred to ride in my Vauxhall to his little 1936 Morris 8. The roads in Northern Ireland, at that time, anyway, were very bumpy and he thought my car would be kinder to his pregnant wife. Consequently, my car was used by them for outings to Belfast, the Giants' Causeway etc.

Yvonne and I, alone this time, had an enjoyable visit to Dublin for which road journey I had to affix GB plates, front and back on my Vauxhall DAD 587. We stayed at the Hibernian Hotel which was a very pleasant experience. The bedroom however had a sloping floor towards the street but for all that the Hibernian was one of the leading hotels and enjoyed a great reputation.

ABOVE: Harry Coldbeck signs the visitors' book in the Lord Mayor of Birmingham's (Alderman E.W. Apps) office on becoming the Station Commander of RAF Castle Bromwich in 1956.

BELOW: RAF Benson's Gate Guard in 1985 was a Spitfire PR.19, the last of the PR Spitfires. The author flew this type in 1948.

ABOVE: This Mk IX Spitfire was Gate Guard at RAF Castle Bromwich in 1956. It is now in the Birmingham Museum of Science and Industry.

Her Majesty Queen Elizabeth II being greeted by Yvonne Coldbeck when she visited RAF Castle Bromwich in 1957. Station Commander Harry Coldbeck looks on.

ABOVE: This photo was taken at RAF Castle Bromwich after the Queen had landed there in 1957.
Left to right: Squadron Leader B.E. Hogan, OC Birmingham University Air Squadron, the author when Station Commander, Air Commodore E. Fielden, Captain of the Queen's Flight, the navigator of the Heron shown in the background and Squadron Leader B. Stanbridge, the pilot.

ABOVE: A photo taken in 1985 of my sleeping quarters in Malta at Siggiewi Signal Station, and (*left*) how it looked in 1942.

1992 – Italian Admiral Mecurio presents the author with a plaque to commemorate his second visit to Augusta in Sicily after fifty years.

The model of a Spitfire PR IV that the author presented to the museum in Augusta to commemorate his visit and in the background the plaque he received in return.

Following my absence from Ulster in England, at the OATS Course, I was again required to travel across the Irish Sea to take part in route-lining in London for the Queen's Coronation. There was a special training period at RAF Cranwell with the specially kitted out flights of airmen. Then near the eve of the Coronation we were required to sleep in Hyde Park in tents. Yvonne, who meanwhile had come over from Ulster, found a helpful policeman who escorted her to the spot in Oxford Street where I and my 'troop' were street-lining. This was quite a remarkable happening considering the huge crowds assembled along the routes.

Towards the end of my year at Cluntoe, I was posted to HQ Bomber Command at RAF High Wycombe in Buckinghamshire as a Staff Officer. This post was labelled O.Est.2*, to take up my promotion to Squadron Leader. We had meantime, however, found a house in Cookstown, in Ireland, belonging to an Irish doctor which was acceptable to Air Ministry as a 'hiring'. This made much more sense, as it was modern and well equipped. Yvonne and dog Derry, stayed with this new accommodation where we entertained our various friends from home and overseas, while I found a new abode in England which was a romantically sounding Cherry Tree Cottage in Speen Bottom, Buckinghamshire.

Up until now, I had shifted us in my car but now our increased time married was reflected in the accumulation of personal goods and chattels. After obtaining the required three quotes, as per Air Ministry instructions, the hired carrier arrived. Looking over the readied belongings, he pointed to the drinks cupboard remnants and said, 'I'm not taking that', in his best Calvinistic tone and that was that. I had to hurriedly deposit it with my friends as we had a boat to catch.

The stevedores at Belfast, where I had previously despatched the car, invited me to stay in it as the crane swung the car up and over onto the deck of the ship. I had then to return to Cookstown by bus to collect Yvonne. A friend had kindly offered to run us to the departure quay at Belfast along with dog Derry and all our personal, last minute baggage. We were slightly disconcerted when he turned up with his girl friend whom he had invited along for the ride. We eased ourselves into the small, two door Anglia car which we now discovered was to be our transport. Our dog had not proved to be a very docile car traveller and I

---

* A post concerned with establishments, responsible for determining personnel requirements required to meet a unit's task.

had to nurse him apprehensively all the way to Belfast, although I was spared his usually inevitable car sickness. That was until we boarded the train at Liverpool which was only slightly less embarrassing.

CHAPTER THIRTEEN

FINAL PHASE

At the Headquarters Bomber Command Admin. Wing, RAF High Wycombe, where my O.Est.2 job was located, I found my future boss was a New Zealand RAF Wing Commander. While I was introducing myself he startled me with, 'All right, get your coat off and we'll get something done!' which rather cut across the usual introductory niceties. He had been a victim of Poliomyelitis in somewhere like Rhodesia and his wife of the time had succumbed to it. It had left him lame with a calliper on one leg and I later realised, other frailties existed. He now had a new charming wife.

We had barely settled into Cherry Tree Cottage when Yvonne complained of the water taps feeling 'slippery'. When I felt them they seemed alright but later when she was standing on the edge of the bath, changing a light bulb, I was steadying her and felt a tingling from her stocking-clad legs which gave rise to some ribald laughter. However, while Yvonne was preparing breakfast, next morning, I was having a shave in the bathroom and with one hand on the tap, I dipped my razor in the basin and the latter was flung across the room. It happened that my Wing Commander had loaned me a volt meter for quite a different reason so I put one electrode on the tap and another on the outlet whereupon it registered 240 volts! We had the telephone on, so we informed Aylesbury power authority after which I switched off the power at the mains and departed for the office. In the evening, Yvonne reported that a man had been to check, but could find nothing wrong although commenting, as he departed, that he would not like to live there! While we were contemplating that, the phone rang. The Supervisor, this time, who said he did not like the sound of what he had been told and could he make another call at the house. Most certainly he could! While he was on the way, some discussion revealed that the strange electrical phenomena manifested itself around meal times – further volt meter tests were negative with the stove off. This helped the supervisor when he arrived to proclaim that the earthing of the stove through the self-contained water system had broken down, causing all the plumbing to be live when the stove was in use! Our landlady had a new stove installed.

The next big event at delightful Cherry Tree Cottage was the High Wycombe Station Commander offering me a brand-new married quarter, which no one else wanted at that time. We accepted with alacrity. Straight out of the builders' hands, this meant a lot of cleaning up but it was heaven to be in this brand-new four bedroom abode.

Our daughter, Susan, was born at Princess Mary Hospital, Halton, on 18 July 1954. I had been along to see them both and on my return, the American Major next door, on an exchange posting, had asked me in for a celebratory drink. I retired to bed, in our quarters, and was sound asleep upstairs when I sensed a commotion outside and the bedroom ceiling was illuminated. On looking outside, I saw the camp fire-engine and a ladder was being placed at our window. I went downstairs and they told me I had not responded to the knocking on the front door and they, the fire service, had been sent by the orderly officer because 'Halton', (Princess Mary Hospital), had requested I be informed my wife was very ill. I threw on my clothes and in the early morning light, I dashed off to the hospital. Fortunately, meanwhile, Yvonne had turned the corner and while deathly pale, was now out of the danger which had threatened.

While at HQ Bomber Command I was able to keep my hand in by flying at Booker, an RAF airfield towards Reading, where as staff officers, we were entitled to fly aircraft on the establishment of HQBC Communications Flight. The flight at that time was commanded by Squadron Leader George Bates, the C-in-C's pilot who lived next door to us at 'Greenwood Site', with his wife and small daughter. In order to keep our Instrument Flight Ratings current, and passing the Green Card flying test every six months, instrument flying was, therefore, high on our priorities.

While on the administration staff of establishments, we were required, from time-to-time, to undertake 'on-site reviews' of the requirements of Bomber Stations and other Bomber Command units. This also applied to various signals units on the Continent. One such unit was established at Wildenrath, in Germany. We carried out a review there in company with the Air Ministry finance member for Bomber Command, travelling there in an Anson of the Communications Flight and staying over the two nights and returning the same way. This was the first time I had been in Germany since I was a POW there and I was amazed at the obvious recovery in the ten years which had elapsed.

The Cold War was obviously behind our signals establishments in Germany.

During the latter end of my second year at Bomber Command and after my experience of the vagaries of postings at Feltwell, and my summary despatch to Northern Ireland, I responded readily when the P2 Squadron Leader enquired about my preference for posting at the end of my tour. My natural choice was for a flying job. It seems he had a Flight Commander's post for a Squadron Leader in a Canberra Squadron in Germany available, so I jumped at the chance.

There was a medical required, before I went back on flying and on jet aircraft, which revealed my hernia problem had resurfaced. The HQBC Medical Staff recommended I have it repaired again before I took up this posting. I was admitted to 'Princess Mary' RAF Hospital and allocated a bed, oddly enough, in the same ward Yvonne had been in when Susan arrived. This was because of re-decorating or other building adjustments.

Recovery from my operation was underway when I learned that my post on Canberras in Germany had been dis-established and the Squadron was now a one flight Squadron such as the 540 PR Mosquito Squadron I had left so reluctantly, at Benson, about seven years earlier. It seemed that flying posts were becoming increasingly scarce. The HQBC P2 Sqn Ldr, Ted Edwards, said he had secured for me a Station Commander's post at RAF Castle Bromwich, on the perimeter of Birmingham City.

CB it transpired was a Home Command flying station which therefore required a General Duties officer as CO on the Station. Located on the Station was the University of Birmingham Air Squadron, commanded by Squadron Leader Hogan and equipped with de Havilland Chipmunks. Dick Hogan obligingly acted as my deputy, formally taking over the Station when I was absent for other duties or on leave. He had other GD officers among his staff, instructors who could deputise for him and it was most convenient for me to hand over to such an officer who knew the form so well.

Another flying unit on the Station was an Air Observation Post, (AOP) Flight which was commanded by an Army Captain who was out of line at times. The Auster aircraft of the AOP Flight and the Chipmunk aircraft of the University Squadron were serviced by Airwork Ltd, which was managed by a very co-operative New Zealander, Noel Cresswell. The AOP flight enjoyed the services of a Master Pilot flying instructor on their strength. Other lodger units

141

on the Station included an RAF Police District HQ commanded by a Wing Commander Worthing and an Auxiliary Air Force Signals Unit commanded by a Wing Commander Glover. An Air Training Corps Wing Commander completed the trio of Wing Commanders.

When I arrived at Castle Bromwich, to take over as Station Commander, the outgoing CO informed me he had recently processed a Redress of Grievance, made by the Police District second-in-command, a Squadron Leader, against his CO the Wing Commander. One day, some time later, I was informed by a Police District spokesman that his CO was on his way down to 'break the Station Commander's head' (mine), because of my predecessor having forwarded the redress confidentially to Group HQ. I followed the AOC's advice when I contacted him, and the matter was fortunately settled outside my field of vision.

The Signals Unit, also a lodger unit, had rules of their own too and this was most obvious in connection with a social club which had a bar in one of the buildings they occupied. It transpired that the Signals Corporal, on the staff of my Station establishment, had, among his number of children, a mentally deficient girl. It appears he had been awarded a compassionate posting to the Birmingham area on this account. It was also subsequently revealed that the Corporal was employed by the Auxiliary Air Force Signals Unit as a part-time barman, at functions which the AAFSU held in their social club, outside normal Station working hours. These social functions gave rise to various complaints from Station personnel regarding noise and other misdemeanours associated with intoxication. Eventually, the Police District became involved and it was decided to do an audit of the offending club. It was found that stocks were seriously astray. In some instances, for example, the front row of full bottles had been counted disguising the several rows of empty ones standing behind them. At the resulting Court Martial, the compassionate side of the Corporal's posting was given much prominence. The Clerk of Works became involved because the terrible state of the Corporal's married quarter, which he occupied with his wife and children, was revealed. Eventually, the Corporal was gaoled and later moved to another station in the area but not before an example of his unsavoury case was made. After which, the clean up could begin. This incorporated action by Social Workers, (SAAFI), in sorting out the tangled finances of the family which included disposing of duplicated pieces of furniture and embodied the paying off of the child's pram, which likewise, was on hire purchase. Subsequently, a new pram was seen being used by the wife and it transpired that the one which had been paid off for them had been sold for cash and a new one obtained on hire purchase!

Another compassionate posting on my staff concerned an Irishman who was addicted to strong drink and when in that state, he would break into places on the Station. One such episode involved the Birmingham police telephoning me in the middle of the night to report that this chap had rammed one of our trucks, stolen from our MT yard, into a street post. Would we kindly collect the truck and the miscreant and deal with the latter appropriately. In his defence, I suppose it must be said, that this airman, when not affected by alcohol was a good if unskilled worker on his compassionate posting.

At other times, the NAAFI was broken into and theft was committed. I do not think the Service Police ever solved these burglaries. In this connection, there was never a dull moment! It was like constantly sitting on a bed of hot coals.

Another interesting and pleasant event, was the visit, in passing, of HM The Queen and HRH the Duke of Edinburgh. It was not a visit to the Station, as such, but to the Rover Scout Moot being held in Sutton Park. The Queen had elected to fly up from London in one of her aircraft of the Queen's Flight, which was a de Havilland Heron. On board was the Captain of the Queen's Flight, Air Commodore Sir Edward Fielden and I discovered the pilot was an old course mate of mine from CFS – I see, incidentally, that nowadays, he is listed in retirement, as Sir Brian Stanbridge, KCVO, CBE, AFC, Air Vice-Marshal, retired. The local Member of Parliament and the Chief of Police, Mr Stanley were present to shake the Royal hands. As well, the Lord Lieutenant of Warwickshire, Lord Willoughby de Brooke was there, among other things, to make the introductions which included the Station Commander and Mrs Coldbeck!

The Queen's aircraft, whilst at Castle Bromwich, was turned around and serviced, on the ground by Airwork Ltd which Company was under the urbane management of Noel Cresswell. This organisation was responsible for the safety and other services, i.e. ambulance, fire-engines, signal square and Air Traffic Control including airfield inspection. The maintenance on the airfield and Station itself, was in the hands of the Clerk of Works and the Station Engineer who had their respective areas of responsibility. In this connection, these gentlemen had to be consulted closely during preparations for the Battle of Britain Open Day in September each year when we received 120,000 patrons in 1956 and 110,000 in 1957.

During the preparations, I was given the temporary establishment of one extra officer and some other ranks, but most of the work devolved onto the Station staff and parented units. Conferences were held on site with the Birmingham Chiefs of the Fire Service, Chief Constable and his staff, the Transport Authorities of Rail and Road as well as the Ambulance and first aid organisations. There was no extra finance available, officially, for the out-goings in connection with the preparations for the 'At Home'. Ice cream vendors and other food licensees provided some funds but it had also become the custom of the various corporations in the locality to advertise in our programme. The compilations and publishing of the programme was undertaken gratis by a Castle Bromwich enthusiast. In connection with all these activities there was a large amount of polite correspondence required, soliciting and acknowledging contributions to the RAF Benevolent Fund.

Squadron Leader Dick Hogan, each year, took up the post of OC Flying and was of tremendous strength in the side. He controlled all the complex comings and goings of the visiting aircraft programme as well as the cruising formations and singles which, while giving demonstrations, did not land at Castle Bromwich. At the end of a very busy day the flying programme, under Dick's management, went without incident during my two hectic years of Battle of Britain 'At Home' days there.

In preparing for the influx of the thousands of visitors, it was necessary to erect rope barriers around the areas where the public were to be accommodated. Included were separate public lavatories for men and for women. A technique had evolved where holes were drilled in the surface of the ground which would take a dustbin receptacle in each. To drill these holes a motorised earth auger was hired and employed. Before each day's drilling commenced, Flight Sergeant Parry, (Station Warrant Officer), who was in charge of these operations, would consult with the Station Engineer about underground cables, drains etc. On one day, the SE indicated by a line on the surface where an underground electricity cable lay and as a result our auger team proceeded to bore their holes elsewhere. My first indication of trouble was when Mr Cammack who ran a Naval Establishment in the 'Spitfire Hangar', so named because it was the scene of the final assembly of some 11,000 Spitfires during the war, rang me to say he had had to send all his female hands home because his electricity was off. Did we know anything about it? He knew his underground mains cable came from our side. Reaching for my cap, I drove my service Vanguard to where I thought the team would be working. They had stopped drilling with the earth auger because of the rain. Flight Sergeant Parry assured me he had requested directions from the Station Engineer about where he could drill. When the rain stopped, investigation revealed that the earth auger had in fact pierced the outer covering of an 11,000 volt cable. Rainwater had then penetrated the cable, luckily after the team had left the drilling scene to take shelter. It was obviously a lucky escape. A Court of Enquiry followed, without the blame being fully resolved.

Having taken every precaution and followed all the rules and regulations, it was always a great relief when the Battle of Britain 'At Home' Day at Castle Bromwich was over. On both the years, 1956 and 1957, when I was in the responsible position of being the Station Commander, my luck held with the September weather, for one thing, and there were no serious accidents, for another, either concerning the massed crowds of over a hundred thousand people, or in the air. It was always a popular occasion apparently with plenty of refreshments such as ice cream, soft drinks, pies etc, for the thousands of spectators. They used to walk the grass off the surface of the soil.

During the build up to what was the second of my Castle Bromwich Battle of Britain 'At Home' Days, this one, September, 1957, I was made aware, in strict confidence, by group HQ that the Station would be closing down during the following year, 1958. There was also another serious matter, which had attracted my attention. An Air Ministry Order (AMO) had been issued, as a result of Mr Duncan Sandys's White Paper on the reduction of the strength of the Air Force, an Air Force which had been built up again during the post war period. Now that electronic guided missiles and an establishment of fewer aircraft, each requiring fewer crew members, were the mode, the costly expansion of numbers of flying personnel was about to be reversed.

One aspect of this reduction in strength was to offer permanent career officers, like myself, in certain older age groups, the chance of early retirement, on a voluntary basis. This early retirement was to be pensionable, in the usual way for career officers. A final gratuity would be paid as well as our repatriation rights being honoured. I was still an active pilot, with no medical or other restrictions, but it was an accepted fact that there was now a surplus of pilots. My flying, since my active post-war operational flying days at Benson, and instructional flying at CFS, Feltwell and Cluntoe was now, apart from a Meteor conversion course, mainly limited to keeping my instrument rating alive. My next posting after CB was anyone's guess and whilst playing about flying Chipmunks on an ad hoc basis was fun, it indicated to me

145

a tapering off of my serious flying days, which was now forecast by the number of my contemporaries filling adjutant and other admin. posts unrelated to rank, experience or training.

Officers who had reached the rank where they would not be usually considered for promotion at that time, generally received a notice to that effect. I had not been so advised and therefore I could still, in theory, expect promotion. I had, however, received encouraging requests to return home to New Zealand, most of which, in the event, turned out to be entirely misleading worthless promises and misguided patriotism. Another factor was my wife had been advised that the health of her mother in New Zealand was causing concern. The voyage to New Zealand still took at least four weeks by ship to traverse the globe from the UK to the 180th Meridian and it was not possible for various reasons, to just nip home with my wife and daughter, Susan, to 'test the water'. In the event, I decided, with reluctance and regretfully, to volunteer under the terms of the AMO to end my active service. This coincided with the closing down of Castle Bromwich in mid 1958.

As a part of the closure, the Birmingham University Air Squadron, under its Commanding Officer, Squadron Leader B.E. Hogan, was moved to RAF Shawbury also in the Midlands and Dick kindly offered me the job of ferrying the final Chipmunk to leave Castle Bromwich for its new home. That too, was my final flight under my own hand in the United Kingdom, mid 1958.

Another small final duty of mine concerned the Mark IX Spitfire which was our Gate Guardian at RAF Castle Bromwich. It stood patiently and unmolested at the gate on its little plot opposite the Guard-room. Once a year, normally, we wheeled it down to the large hangar, before Battle of Britain Day, for a touch up and general clean and as far as I could tell it was complete. Quite a lot of people liked looking at it and photographing it. One enthusiast made a small model of it and sent it to me anonymously.

As soon as it became known that the Station was closing, I received numerous applications from other stations and individuals as well as firms, to take over the Spitfire. One application which appealed to me however was from the Birmingham Museum of Science and Industry.

When the Air Ministry asked me for my recommendation for its disposal, I had no hesitation in advocating the Birmingham Museum of Science and Industry, where it would be cared for properly under cover and would survive within the City which had been its birthplace along with approximately eleven thousand others! Originally Mark

IX ML 427, it was, at one time, re-categorised to 6547 M, as an instructional airframe. In 1954, as ML 427, it was allocated to RAF Castle Bromwich as a Gate Guardian. In 1958, Air Ministry allotted it to the Birmingham Museum where it remains today bearing the letters A ST.

Introduction to the Malta of 1941

By Flight Lieutenant Jim Berrett MID, RAFVR

This is an introduction to the violent and devastating theatre of war which Harry entered when he arrived in Malta in March 1942. It is also an introduction to No. 69 Squadron, RAF, which, before Harry's arrival, carried on doing its job of photographic and general reconnaissance, whatever the odds, throughout the siege of the Island.

In August 1940, consequent upon Italy's entry into the war in June, the Royal Air Force High Command were considering the necessity of keeping a reconnaissance unit in the central Mediterranean in order to monitor the Italian fleet and other shipping movements. Malta, almost 1000 miles from the friendly bases, Gibraltar in the west and Alexandria in Egypt, was the only possible choice for a reconnaissance base in spite of the fact that hostile Sicily, with all its aerodromes, was only 60 miles to the north.

Accordingly, 22 Squadron in England, was asked to evaluate the qualities of a recently-produced American attack-bomber, the Glenn Martin 167F. They were given three aircraft all of which had originally been destined for the French Air Force and which, on the fall of France, the RAF had obtained for Allied use. The fact that, in the early stages, aircraft and flying manuals were annotated in French made assessment difficult.

Flight Lieutenant 'Titch' Whiteley was given the original job of evaluation and setting up 431 GR Flight. He found the aircraft was an excellent performer and at certain heights could outstrip a Hurricane I – a valuable speed asset when it came to avoiding Italian fighters.

The 431 Reconnaissance Flight constituted ex-members of 22 Squadron and the original plan was to send three of these aeroplanes flying direct to Malta followed by three more at a later date when additional crews had adapted to the new aircraft which was, in due course, officially named the Maryland after its American State of origin.

In September 1940 the three Marylands successfully flew direct to Malta and the crews were very quickly into a regular round of photographing Italian ports from Naples in the north to Tripoli in the south.

They very quickly made a name for themselves, persevering, getting their aerial pictures and contributing vital knowledge of naval and merchant shipping movements. In addition, watch was kept on enemy aerodromes, many of which were but a short distance from Luqa, Malta. The Maryland's speed was often a factor in successfully avoiding enemy fighters.

In November 1940 photographs taken of Taranto made headlines when Fleet Air Arm Swordfish, operating from the carrier HMS *Illustrious* sank and damaged vital Italian naval vessels. The Swordfish used these reconnaissance photographs before and after the attack.

Three additional Maryland crews, meanwhile, were training in England and Ireland and in due course, were ready to fly direct to Malta. One crew crashed on a training flight in Ireland and another was lost on the way to Malta. The other crew however, after two months flying and becoming accustomed to the well-liked Maryland, was ready to fly direct to Malta. Flying this strange machine around a trigger-happy Britain had been, at times, hazardous. Many signals were sent warning fighter groups and AA emplacements of the possible appearance of the Marylands.

In the early morning of 19 December 1940, a course was set direct to Malta from Thorney Island. At this time there was a great shortage of Marylands and their spare parts. These were crammed in with supplies and were met at Luqa some seven hours twenty minutes later by an enthusiastic band of technicians – not for personal attendance there but for those precious spares which were carried by the new arrival.

When the Marylands arrived they joined the regular coverage of enemy ports and aerodromes. Between Italy's declaration of war, and the above arrival, the Island had been subject to 211 air raids by Italian bombers and fighters. The Italians were not quite as intrepid as the *Luftwaffe* nevertheless there was much damage done and many civilian casualties by the end of 1940.

On 10 January 1941, 431 GR Flight became 69 Squadron – a squadron which was originally formed in the First World War. Of far greater significance was the fact that *Luftwaffe* squadrons were now established in Sicily. We first became aware of this when news came through that the Royal Navy's carrier, HMS *Illustrious* had been attacked and the enemy aircraft had done enormous damage to the ship. Two days later a similar raid was made on Luqa airfield. Many major raids followed and yet the Island managed to keep its composure and folk went about their business perhaps with an ear cocked for the regular air raid warnings.

Flying from and returning to base became more hazardous in daylight with the advent of Me 109s. No. 69 Squadron, still short of aeroplanes and aircrew, managed to fulfil its commitments, unfortunately with regular losses.

Heavy day and night raids on Malta continued until the end of May 1941 when the *Luftwaffe* was withdrawn from Sicily for duty on the Russian Front. Night raids became heavier from the Italians but there was certainly a respite in daytime.

The squadron was having great success photographing ports and airfields and particularly in finding and shadowing enemy convoys which were then heavily attacked by Blenheim IVs of 2 Group, Swordfish of the Fleet Air Arm (based at Halfar), submarines and task forces of Royal Navy cruisers and destroyers. Rommel, in North Africa, lost many supplies on their way from Italy to North Africa. Sea reconnaissance was so busy and aircraft were in such short supply, that 69 Squadron found it necessary to borrow and use Blenheim IVs from other units for a short time in September. During September, October and November many enemy ships were found and sunk.

It appears the *Luftwaffe* considered that this success could not be allowed to continue, for the enemy returned in force at the beginning of December 1941. In a period of $11\frac{1}{2}$ months there had been 812 air raids on the Island. There was much worse to come. The Axis made as many as 400 sorties against the Island in one day and in April 1942, the enemy dropped 6728 tons of bombs on Malta.

Whilst there had been an influx of Marylands and aircrew reinforcements from the Middle East it was becoming more and more difficult for these twin-engined bombers to operate. Losses, particularly around the Island, were becoming unsustainable.

Meanwhile a Hurricane had earlier been tried for photographic purposes with some success. Then in March 1942, Harry Coldbeck arrived in the maelstrom that was Malta with his PRU Spitfire. For a time he did all the photographic reconnaissance sorties. The role of the Marylands was greatly diminished by 1942.

In this situation, Harry with his Spitfire AB300, was the sole operator of Photographic Reconnaissance from Malta. This entailed Harry flying many hundreds of miles over the sea, alone, in an un-armed aircraft, to obtain daily aircraft counts on enemy airfields and the shipping occupancy of selected harbours. The return was made to a dangerous island and life on the ground.

A summary of Harry Coldbeck's operations from Malta is at the Appendix to this Annex.

ANALYSIS OF H. COLDBECK'S OPERATIONS FROM MALTA 13.3.42–10.11.42

Total operations	153

Comprising
Photo-reconnaissance	80
Photo-reconnaissance and Navy/convoy search	70
Visual reconnaissance	3

Flew 2 sorties in a day 18 times

Operated on 15 consecutive days
18 September to 2 October 1942

Encountered fighters 8 times
and heavy ack-ack 13 times

SUMMARY

1942

	Photo-Recce	Photo-Recce Navy/Convoy	Visual Recce	Fighters	AA	Times 2 Sorties in 1 Day	Total
Mar	4			1	2		4
Apr	12				1		12
May	16					2	16
June	10	12	2	1		5	24
July	7	12		1	3	2	19
Aug	11	14		2		3	25
Sept	8	17	1	1	2	3	26
Oct	8	9		2	2		17
Nov	4	6			3	3	10
	80	70	3	8	13	18	153

MALTA RE-VISITED – 1985

After my retirement I had often thought about Malta, Italy and the Mediterranean generally. By the time 1985 arrived I had enquired of various travel agencies about programmed tours to Southern Italy/Sicily and Malta. The invariable New Zealand answer at that time was that that sort of trip would have to be sought and arranged in the UK.

I had not been back to Malta or Italy and I did not know anyone there so I decided to set off for England under the auspices of my daughter Susan's Pan Am connections. At the same time I could take up a long standing invitation from June Rees, an old family friend, to visit them. Meanwhile, June had decided to take off for her annual visit to her offspring in the Antipodes. My departure from New Zealand was delayed for various reasons and in the end, my potential hostess June was arriving at Auckland Airport literally as I was departing. June gave me the telephone numbers to ring to contact her 'Majordomo' Terry Richardson who would pick me up at Heathrow where the aircraft was landing.

The pick-up was duly carried out by Terry and her husband, David and I was installed, heavily jet-lagged, at June's house, 'Scarletts Acre', near Newbury in Berkshire. Terry had arranged to leave me some eggs and other breakfast items for when I surfaced in the morning.

Next day David, Terry's husband contacted me and with his son Richard aged twelve he motored me in June's car up to Old Warden aerodrome where we had a wonderful time inspecting all the aircraft on display on the ground and in the air. These included the Bristol Fighter F2B, Hawker Hart, Gloster Gladiator, Gipsy Moth (DH60) and Supermarine Spitfire. Afterwards we visited the RAF Museum at Hendon with all the beautiful specimens on view; then to RAF Benson, where I had been stationed several times in war and peace, flying PR Spitfires and PR Mosquitoes. The gate guardian was a beautifully maintained PR Spitfire 19, standing in its plot with an inscribed plate recording the squadrons and groups which took part in photographic reconnaissance and remembering the pilots who failed to return.

I took photographs at each of these three places. At Benson, I asked the corporal in the guardroom if it was permissible. He replied, 'Only the Spitfire aircraft – not down the station road.' which incidentally led to the hangars.

Arriving back at 'Scarletts Acre', after a great feast of interesting scenes and aircraft, we found June's husband, Neville, entertaining some friends to drinks to which we were cordially invited. Neville returned to London leaving instructions as to how I would be put on the train for Victoria next day, with directions to find the Rees flat in Greystones Street, Victoria.

Having taken my leave of the very kind Richardsons, I made my way from Victoria Station along Victoria Road, passing the well-known person of ex-Premier Harold Wilson, who was walking back towards the station. Neville had left a note for me with clear instructions on how to gain admission to the flat. We enjoyed a wonderful dinner, after his return that evening. Next day it was down to Malta Air to book a seat to Luqa. Alas, no seats were available for the duration of my stay! In response to my request for help, in the limited time available to me, the counter girl suggested I try an address in Soho, which she gave me. After ploughing my way through the barrow vendors and general exotica of Soho, I found the address I had been given. Inside the premises I was issued with a ticket, for an unbelievably moderate sum, which I was assured would provide me with three nights' bed and breakfast and a return trip to Luqa with British Airways Holidays! When I told Neville about my experience he exclaimed, 'That was a bucket shop!'

The flight originated at Gatwick and so I boarded the express train at convenient Victoria Station. Our departure was scheduled for late afternoon and the sun was shining as we all took our seats in the full-to-capacity airliner. All the preliminaries had been completed when an official announced that as they couldn't get the door to shut completely we would all have to disembark for an hour or so until a new one was fitted. It seemed to be all of that time before we were allowed back. As it was completely dark before we finally took off there was no hope of seeing anything of my familiar Mediterranean haunts.

Arrival at Luqa, Malta, was quite late, around midnight, and after the usual disembarkation procedures I walked out to find a man displaying a card over his head with COLDBECK in large letters on it. The Maltese man said he had been waiting a long time and invited me to join some others, apparently from the same flight, already seated in his vehicle. Eventually I was the last to be dropped off and the man, who was also the driver, took me to the Capua Court Hotel which was closed for the night. The driver had a key, however, and knew which room to place me into. He was then gone in a flash. The bedroom in the limestone rock was small and somewhat like I imagined a cell would be.

In the morning I was hungry and thirsty. In the dining-room I asked for bacon and eggs which other guests appeared to be enjoying. Oh no, just Continental breakfast, a roll and coffee for me even when I was offering to pay extra if that was what was required. Apparently I had ended up in Sliema, so first thing after consuming my roll I made my way to Valletta and took one of the taxis to the airport at Luqa. How things had changed. I could not recognise anything. I asked a few people if any wartime buildings remained but they just looked uncomprehendingly and said they did not know. I suppose fifty years or so is outside the younger generation's interest.

Up in the passenger lounge which I had entirely to myself there was a great view right across the airfield. I noticed I was under surveillance by a uniformed man in a peaked cap so I approached him and mentioned my wartime association with Luqa in 1942. He listened politely, cancelled his scrutiny of me and I was on my own again.

On the way back to Valletta, this time on foot, I walked past the 'Poorhouse' – a well known large building in which mainly aircrew were quartered at least during 1942 when I was in Malta. The place was much the same as I remembered it but it seemed to be further back from the road, although I never knew it very well or intimately. Back in Valletta I looked in on the War Museum where the kindly curator showed me a few bits and pieces of aeroplanes, (including some of the Gladiator), and water craft. He also pointed out photographs on the wall of various prominent wartime personalities. Also on the museum wall I recognised an aerial photograph of Takali, April 1942, which I had taken, showing war damage. I enquired about a ferry trip to Augusta and gathered it was the wrong day and anyway, as the ferry went to Syracuse, I would have to find transport on land to Augusta. Not enough time. Eventually I made my way back, looking at the shops, to my little room where from next day, after another fruitless attempt to have a 'proper' breakfast, I set off for Takali. In the area, where Takali airfield used to be, I discovered vegetation and quasi-industrial buildings, so I moved on up to the high ground of Mdina. At the *Point de Vue* restaurant there I had a pleasant meal looking out over the area I had contemplated with such awe with

Luqa away on the right taking terrible punishment from the Ju 88s. This, when I first arrived in my blue Spitfire AB300, 7 March 1942. It was up here, too, that the kindly Intelligence Officer had told me it had been decreed I would stay on Malta, instead of proceeding to the Middle East. Unfortunately he was killed in one of the intense bombing raids on the area, apparently in reply by the enemy to the introduction of the Spitfires operating from Takali, in mid-March. Stumbling back along the dusty roads, keeping out of the way of the passing cars, eventually I caught a bus and was once again in Valetta where I waited for the bus to Siggiewi. After asking for assurance that I was waiting in the right bus place, an elderly man was most responsive and reassured me I was on the right track.

Upon arrival at Siggiewi, my new-found guide pointed out the unmarked road to the Signal Station, where I had lived during my entire time, in 1942, at Luqa. Before we parted he knocked on his own door and asked a young female relative for a pencil and paper upon which we exchanged names and addresses. After goodbyes, I set off down the country road which I had not known previously because I had always approached the Signal Station from the airfield itself, which is on the other side of the Signal Station. On the way, some agricultural-type workers passed me in wheeled vehicles giving me enquiring looks as they motored along. I imagined I was well off the usual tourist track, on foot with my camera. The rusty aerial towers, which looked like the original ones I remembered from fifty years ago, came into view and the building which looked like the one in which I slept during the eight months or so was now behind a high security wire-netting fence. My elderly informant had told me the area was now a police training school. The weather was now deteriorating, so I took some photos and as it seemed to me to be threatening to rain I decided to beat a retreat and return along the country roadway to Siggiewi where I could catch a bus back to Valetta.

On my eventual return to New Zealand I wrote to Mr Valentine, my Siggiewi guide, to thank him for his help. I also sent him pictorial cards of New Zealand which he had requested. Christmas cards too, for some years, were exchanged but they too faded out.

My flight back to Gatwick from Malta started in the small hours of the third morning and we again crossed the areas I had hoped to see but as in the outward trip, it was in darkness. I was, however, reminded of my 'hour before first light' adventures of back in 1942. Well into our flight, the Captain informed us that we had been diverted to Heathrow but that transport would be laid on to take us back to Gatwick. I did not really need to return to Gatwick but I enjoyed the bus ride as a sight-seeing venture before I caught the express train back to Victoria. I walked comfortably on to Neville's flat, where his warm hospitality was once more enjoyed.

Back in London I called my old friend Laddie Lucas, at his residence and discovered his wife, Jill, was in hospital, undergoing a serious operation. But Laddie made an half hour available to me. We enjoyed a cup of tea which he had brewed for us as we discussed the past, the present and some future. I took some photos. The phone was demanding his attention quite a lot of the time but I was delighted to have made personal contact with him after about forty years.

For the trip home I was booked on one of the last of the Pan American flights to New Zealand, before that Company closed. It was scheduled to leave Heathrow and fly non-stop to San Francisco. As its departure was fairly early Dr Neville Rees, my host, decided to take me by car to the departure point in spite of the traffic congestion he would have to face on his return. We could see some of the intense traffic mass on the opposite side of our motorway as we proceeded to Heathrow.

The aircraft departure from the loading point was slightly delayed, because an elderly passenger had dropped his duty-free bottle from the overhead locker onto the head of a woman, of similar age, in the seat below. The unfortunate woman was evacuated by medical people.

For my part, I had been allotted an excellent window seat in the front of the aircraft, (Boeing 747). It was a wonderful day for flying. At the height of thirty thousand feet the views were spectacular and this was particularly enjoyable as we passed Greenland and Iceland in full sunshine.

It had been a short, but delightfully enjoyable visit back to the UK, after an absence of some twenty-seven years. I had also traversed some old tracks on Malta after forty years. Everywhere I had gone many old haunts had disappeared – others were only vaguely recognisable. It was in Malta however that the differences were most marked.

RETURN TO AUGUSTA, SICILY – 1992

I n mid-1985 I had paid my return visit to Malta as detailed in Annex 2 without being able to organise a trip to Augusta. At that time a day trip was out of the question for the ferry service did not allow for that. It was therefore with great elation that in 1988, I received a letter from a Sicilian Historian, Dr Tullio Marcon of Augusta, asking me about my having been shot down, rescued and made a prisoner-of-war at Augusta, on 10 November 1942.

From then on, we had a most interesting correspondence culminating in an invitation from Dr Marcon, to visit his small museum of wartime memorabilia which he had been developing. It was during our correspondence that the doctor showed me the reference of an aerial photograph of Augusta taken on 5 August 1942. After referring to my flying log book, I found that by coincidence, it was one of a series I had taken, in Spitfire BP915. This enabled me to send away to the address provided by Dr Marcon to the Air Photo Library, Dept of Geography, University of Keele, England for a copy of a photo I had taken fifty years previously.

In 1991, I was invited by Laddie Lucas to say whether I would be willing to attend a Malta, (1942) reunion which he was thinking of organising. My reply was an emphatic yes. In the end, the reunion was organised and refreshment and registration fees paid months in advance of the function which was to be held in the RAF Club, London. My daughter, Susan, being at that time, an employee of Continental Airlines, came up with the proposal that I travel to the UK as her free partner for her annual vacation. Also, Alitalia, in Sydney, came up with a concession ticket for me from London to Catania, in Sicily, via Rome.

The trip started from Auckland. We had a most comfortable journey in a Continental Boeing 747, in first class seats, to California. Thence on to Houston, Texas, where we stayed the night in the

Continental airport hotel. I was intrigued by the electric robot train which picked up and dropped off airline passengers and their luggage right inside the hotel. Susan was unable to book us on an early flight from Houston to London next day so she arranged for a transit flight to Newark, New Jersey where we embarked on another Continental 747 for London. We were met at Gatwick by an old friend of my wife's, who took us to her home in Surbiton, Surrey.

From there we phoned Dr Tullio Marcon and a day or so later, boarded an Alitalia aircraft at Heathrow and after a few waits and changes in Rome, we were met by Tullio at Catania, in Sicily. The airport was quite unlike anything I had imagined, for I had previously only viewed it from above in 1942. Tullio greeted us warmly and then motored us to Augusta in his Alfa Romeo. En route, he informed us we were to meet the Admiral currently commanding the Augusta Naval Station at 4 o'clock that day, so he dropped us off at our hotel in Augusta meanwhile to freshen up etc. Prior to our leaving New Zealand, Tullio had warned that the hotel at Augusta was still recovering from the influx of refugees following the severe earthquake at Lentini, on the Catania Plains.

At the appointed time Dr Marcon took us to the office of Admiral Mecurio where the Admiral made a speech of welcome in excellent English, embracing details of my previous 'visit' fifty years ago. The details of my two visits, half a century apart, were engraved on a brass plate beneath the Arms of Augusta, all this mounted on a polished wooden base designed to hang on my wall. This plaque was then presented to me by Admiral Mecurio.

While this ceremony was taking place, Susan was comfortably seated as spectator with Dr Marcon taking photographs. Afterwards, Tullio took Susan and me on a tour of the Naval establishment including the Infirmary where I had been cared for while recovering from my injuries suffered while being forcibly ejected from the Spitfire. We also visited the Augusta railway station where, while waiting with my guards, I had been approached by the Captain of the small steam vessel which first found me in the sea. Dr Marcon then took us in his car on a tour of Augusta itself. This included his pointing out various buildings and shops we had previously discussed by letter. I took photographs of those where the Royal Marines under, (now NZ resident, deceased), Captain Edward Parsons, had established bakeries to help feed the populace after the Allied invasion of Sicily. Tullio still buys his bread from one of these places. On my return to New Zealand, Captain Parsons expressed great pleasure at the sight of the photographs of these premises again.

It was on this sight-seeing trip that I noticed the airship hangar situated on higher ground. Tullio, about a year previously, in 1991, had sent me a card with a pen and ink drawing of this building. It was built in 1917. It is a unique structure of its type in the world, still standing, being constructed of reinforced concrete. It is *Monumento Nazionale dal 1987.*

After this motoring excursion we were entertained to an evening meal at one of Dr Marcon's favourite eating places, right on the edge of the sea, and afterwards he dropped us off at the hotel for the night. Next morning we were up and about early enjoying a splendid bacon and eggs breakfast. I settled our account at the desk where I had, the night before, rescued our passports from the open unattended pigeonhole.

Tullio arrived meanwhile to take Susan and me to Syracuse and was protesting to the hotel staff for accepting our settlement of the bill. He said he had left strict instructions not to accept our payment. Anyway, after thanking him for his potential and actual generosity and hospitality, we set off for Syracuse, passing a War Graves Commission Cemetery where Tullio remarked that Group Captain Walter Churchill was buried there. Tullio left us at a very up-market hotel, 'Agip', the name of which means 'five-legged dog'. Susan and I found out how to get to some of the Greek and some of the Roman Antiquities as well as other geographical features including an echoing chamber, all well patronised by tourists. Tired out in the evening, we were glad of the excellent food in the hotel dining-room and the comfortable beds. Tullio was expecting some important people to see him next day so Susan and I agreed to amuse ourselves. This resulted in my hiring a Fiat Panda with my credit card and Susan drove us to Taormina on the north-east coast of Sicily where we knew there was great scenery to be admired. Unfortunately, that side of Mt Etna was in cloud and we saw very little until we descended out of the cloud again. Susan managed the car and the traffic driving on the right, splendidly. On our return we were quite early so we stopped off at the Cemetery which Tullio had pointed out to us and found the grave of Group Captain Churchill, whom I clearly remembered at Malta. I took some photographs of this very well kept and indexed War Graves Commission cemetery at Syracuse.

Tullio regretted that his important appointment had not materialised and he was also sorry he had not made arrangements to accompany us. However, it was all very interesting on the road navigating ourselves and our general observations of life in Sicily. Next day, Tullio called for us again to take us to Catania in his car, to emplane for Rome and London. On the way and passing Augusta again, the harbour, which I recall once had had cruisers, flying boats and a general Naval air about it, was now dominated by oil tankers and had the general air of an untidy oil port with oil refineries stretching away inland.

At Catania, Tullio said he was not good at goodbyes. It had been a short visit although filled with emotive moments. As detailed in the body of my story, my rescue and subsequent treatment in wartime at Augusta have left me with a warm feeling for the place. I did not see the Rome railway station of previous mention in my story with memories of the kind Italian Major who had provided food and dressings for my head. There were some potentially exciting moments at the airport when a *Carabiniere* twice unfastened his submachine-gun and went to investigate some noisy behaviour. However, that passed over and the London-bound flight was on its way with us two on board. My seated neighbour proved to be a young Alitalia pilot of Italian descent, born in England and now on a re-positioning flight to London. Other Italian passengers expressed interest in our presence with questions they plied us with such as my wartime experiences in their part of the world and the reasons for our visit to Sicily.

Back in Surbiton, Joan took us under her wing again and motored us to visit the RAF married quarters where we had been living at RAF High Wycombe when Susan was born as well as the historic Hughenden Anglican Church where she was christened. Solo, by train, I visited Sutton Coldfield for an overnight stay with Flight Lieutenant Ken Foster of RAF Castle Bromwich days. That Air Force Station is now a gigantic housing estate and although the station commander's married quarters where we lived in 1958 survives, there is little else to be recognised of the old flying station. Everything gone.

Dick Hogan, the one-time Commanding Officer of Birmingham Air Squadron, now living with his wife in Devon, met me at the Honiton railway station. We toured the waterfront then adjourned to a local hostelry to keep an appointment to meet Johnny Bloxham, one time 'Duty Wing Commander' at Luqa. Several Wing Commanders went under that title simultaneously for it was necessary for one of them to be always on duty over the twenty-four hours during the Axis blitz on Malta so as to cope with transit and local flying activity. I was sorry to hear Johnny had lost his son in the Falklands Islands' operations. Next day I farewelled Dick and his wife again. An interval of thirty-four years had elapsed since we all had departed from Castle Bromwich. At Surbiton we farewelled the very kind Joan and took the train to the Armed Servicemens' club in the vicinity of Edgware Road. In New Zealand, I had had to become a financial club member before we left for England. This course of action was recommended by the reunion secretary and had booked in for two nights so that we could attend the reunion next day at the RAF Club. The quarters of the Armed Servicemens' Club were a big disappointment, particularly to my daughter who was expecting something better. There were rough concrete floors in the ablutions, no phones, radio or other means of communication. The ablutions were all down the long corridor from the bedrooms. However we had to make the best of it.

Laddie Lucas had very kindly invited Susan and me along with half a dozen other reunion couples to dinner at his residence in Onslow Square. We had also been invited, through Laddie, to a cocktail party to take place just before his dinner party. Susan had also accepted an invitation to call on an elderly friend whose address we found to be adjacent to the cocktail party address. All three were great occasions and we thoroughly enjoyed the marvellous hospitality. Afterwards, back to our spartan quarters. What a 'let-down.'

Next day, at the Servicemen's Club, Susan was suffering from a severe headache and hoped she was not developing something which would interfere with our schedule of bookings for the return flight homewards next day. In consequence I set off on my own for the reunion, at the RAF Club. As it was raining I left my camera behind, thinking there would be plenty of photographers there. Having put my umbrella in the cloakroom, I found the party room already very full and noisy and while looking around for a familiar face, I was approached by, presumably, a waiter carrying a bottle in each hand who invited me to have a drink. He said, 'You'll have to find a glass first!' There were various young women and young men drifting around through the crowd with plates of what looked like Welsh Rarebit or grilled cheese on pieces of toast which I declined, saying, 'I'll wait for lunch'. 'This is lunch' said one. So, after that incredible statement I saw a plate of sausages in the distance and thought I would have one but it disappeared into the now thick crowd and when I caught up with it, the plate was empty. This was my lunch I had paid for in advance, in New Zealand! Meanwhile I had been 'captured' as it were by one expatriate New Zealander who had been on my Wings course in 1941. He threw his arms around my neck and kept them there as if he was trying to emulate the legendary albatross while his English wife took up a position on the other side of me to ply me with conversation and questions about New Zealand. Fortunately, Les Colquhoun and Jo

163

Dalley, (now Group Captain, Retired), appeared and I was able to dilute the embrace with my reunion with them, after fifty years. Jo told me that with me disappearing that day, 10 November 1942, the newest arrival disappeared also, the newest and oldest in one day, he said, which shook them somewhat. After offering a drink to my old friends, I took myself off to the bar to have at least one set of drinks on my pre-paid reunion refreshment subscription but no, those were on my charge and then the bar closed!

I was wondering about Susan back there in that room, isolated. There was no way of knowing how she was except by going back there and finding out. Someone picked up a bottle and bashed the base hard three times on one of the few tables and another stood up on one of the few chairs. We could tell he was speaking because his lips were moving. The noise and lack of elevation precluded hearing what was being said.

We met a new name, W.A. (Bill) Chawner, from 69 Squadron, who was on ground-crew duties in those days. His wife had a camera and took a photo of him with Les Colquhoun, Jo Dalley and myself. He kindly sent me a print and I had it copied as my sole memento of the occasion. The secretary had promised me a set of names and addresses. These did not eventuate.

After moving around I said goodbye to all I had been reunited with and the few new ones. Finally a last goodbye to Laddie, who, as chairman of the reunion, had been anchored to a table in the corridor apparently by pressure of former comrades wanting to speak with him.

On arrival back at Susan's room, I found her still in bed where she had been all day alone and unattended. I felt so sorry for her. She was however much improved – confident she would be able to catch our scheduled Continental Airline's departure in the morning. Although it was well after mid-afternoon, I went out on the street to a cafe to buy some lunch and some refreshment for Susan. In spite of these vicissitudes our journey across the world from 180 degrees to zero meridian and back again was a well-organised adventure by my daughter. All mainly in first-class travel and hotel accommodation.

REMINISCENCES OF WAR

T he war with its baggage of suffering, adversity and privation will remain for many, who fought and lived in that period, the most important part of their lives. Between the beginning of the war and the end with the approximation of 50 years that have passed, in many it has kindled the desire to see the places where all these things have happened and something that is very important and has remained in the memory of those who have taken part, and this is the case of a NZ pilot who has served in Malta in 1942.

Flying nearly every day, over Naval bases of the Axis, to photograph with his very fast Spitfire – but on 10 Nov. '42, fate wasn't very kind to the then, Flt Lt Coldbeck of 69 Squadron, RAF. A direct hit in the sky of Augusta brought him down, making him fall into the sea in vicinity of Magnisi Peninsula.

Slightly wounded, but with parachute, he fell into the sea. It would be referred to in the Bulletin No. 899 the day after. Having witnessed the episode, the Admiral caused a motor launch to speed out to the open sea and so saved the aviator. It took him to the Infirmary for first aid and afterwards, normal interrogation. The Italians have always been humanitarian towards PoWs, even if it hasn't always worked out that way. The process of interrogation didn't reveal much. It was more important to ready his health for onward journey to prison camp. He was not only given his uniform back, washed and cleaned but also, on the direct intervention of the Admiral, was also given a parcel with useful contents for the journey.

The memory of those days in Augusta was so different from those in Germany till the end of the war, so that many years after warm feelings remained in Coldbeck for the Italians. His desire to re-visit their country persisted so much so that the long trip from NZ (not a light affair), was finally undertaken in 1992, the year of a reunion in London of former Malta's pilots. So, H.C., now a Squadron Leader in retirement, came back to Augusta on 28 April, almost 50 years after his first visit to the town. He re-visited the Naval Base, the Infirmary, the railway station and the other places that occupied so much space in his memory. It was up to Admiral Sergio Mercurio, present day successor of the other Admiral of 1942 period, (a wonderfully caring and benevolent man, in the words of H.C.), to receive the thanks for what the Italian Navy had done at that time for that prisoner. A Crest of Augusta with two dates: 1942–1992, and a shake of the hand concluded this moving meeting.

Nearly a lifetime has sealed this short and significant meeting and apart from the emotion angle, the episode shows how in war, the real values of human solidarity remains alive. So much alive to resist the passing of time.

Tullio Marcon

The above article appeared in the Italian Naval Periodical *Notiziario Della Marina* and was translated from the Italian by the author Dr Tullio Marcon.

ANNEX 5

W hile assembling this book I wrote to Jo Dalley, now Group Captain J. O. Dalley, OBE, DFM, RAF (Retired), in search of photographs covering our joint wartime experiences in 1942 in Malta.

Further correspondence brought forth the following letter which the Group Captain wrote to me. This letter illustrates the sharp memories and sympathy which he retains of the Malta Siege and our involvement in it there.

He also reveals some of the contact, albeit small, which we had with the Maltese civilians in their extremely difficult and hazardous times.

Dear Harry,

Thank you for your letter and returned photos etc. I am deeply sorry that your logbook was not properly made up and all assessments made. I seem to remember the Sqn Adjt collected yours and a Sgt Pilot's (shot down over W Sicily the same afternoon). They both just disappeared. (log books)

Your query re 'The Talisman'. You must well remember our Maltese cleaner, (janitor in the Operations/Intelligence block which included 'the dispersal' 6′ × 8′ – one desk and 2 chairs). He was affectionately known as 'Joe' and would bring his grandson to work with him at Luqa on Saturdays.

After the chocolate was bought from the ship's store of the *Brisbane Star* with Les C's DFM gratuity (£20) we were allocated on repayment, one small chocolate bar per operationally-flown day. We used to pass on some of this chocolate to the grandson on Saturdays. I recall you were particularly precise and generous in this respect.

We also, I believe, had respect for 'Joe'. He always turned up for work on time and was cheerful in spite of the regular bombing. We spoke to him each day and to his grandson on Saturdays.

One or two days after you were shot down, 'Joe' asked where was the New Zealand officer. I seem to remember Les and I were asked when together. We said that sadly you had been shot down over Sicily but were reported alive and a prisoner-of-war. Two enormous tears welled up in his eyes and he turned away. A few minutes later (to allow him to recover) I again spoke to him, put my arm round his shoulder and said 'Please remember it could have been worse – we hope Flt/Lt Coldbeck will return home to his family when the war is over'. A result we never doubted in Malta.

He agreed but was so upset – he remembered that he always felt the three of us represented hope as we were so cheerful and always there every day, month after month.

The next day 'Joe' asked if I would talk to him for a few minutes. I also think he spoke to Les as well. He said that he had spent the previous evening at his local church offering prayers for the three of us and especially the New Zealand officer now in Sicily. He had also sought the assistance and guidance of his priest on how to support us. The priest then produced an elegantly hand-printed short note in Maltese on the very poor quality paper available at the time. He instructed 'Joe' to give it to me personally with the strict instruction to always carry it when flying. The priest assured 'Joe' that if I did this I would be safe. I promised to abide strictly by the guidance given, thanked him for his kindness and that his support meant a great deal – (as indeed it did).

Roughly translated the note said 'May God and the prayers of the Maltese people keep you safe.' It is a very poignant memory, in many ways, is very personal and deeply etched on my memory. I tried to find 'Joe' when I spent a couple of days at Luqa in 1967 but was unsuccessful – he would have been very old by then, if alive.

Strangely, the day after receiving 'The Talisman' my first sortie of the day was to photograph Elmas (Cagliari) and Decimommanu airfields on Sardinia. I noted six MC 202s taking off from Elmas as I completed photographing the airfield and calculated I could also photograph Decimommanu before they could reach me. Decimommanu, you will remember, was a large airfield with highly dispersed bomb-dumps and as I completed the entire photography I realised I had 'cut things a bit fine' as the 202s were about to enter shooting range from below and behind – (watched carefully as I thought in my mirror as they climbed!). After a few twists and turns I managed to reduce the odds by forcing the six 202s into an almost line astern formation and soon after shook them off.

Strangely, this particular episode is recorded by Christopher Shores in his book *Fighters Over Tunisia.* Where he got the information, which is very accurate, I do not know. Either the Italian Air Force or the 69 Sqn combat report I completed on return to Luqa. By the time I left Malta this episode was being circulated in the dispersals as *15* MC 202s attacking Warburton – I never spoke to anyone about this, I was just highly amused.

Your shooting down over Sicily and that of a Sgt Pilot on his first PR sortie with 69 over Western Sicily the same day are also briefly recorded in *Fighters Over Tunisia.*

Needless to say I kept 'The Talisman' in my flying suit until I retired in 1975 by which time it was tattered and unreadable. It saw me through my next operational tour in NW Europe in 1944/45 when I returned to fighters – (No 1 Sqn – Spitfire Mk IX LF (low flying) having contracted 'the bends' rather badly during the last month in Malta – above 27,000ft. 'The bends' finally cleared in 1953, (11 years) when the bubbles disappeared and I was able to pass the decompression tests including explosive decompression tests. 'The Talisman' saw service from the Arctic to Woomera in Australia and safely through one or two nasty experiences over the years.

This sounds all very long-winded but I hope you can pick out any bits you wish to use. I have never outlined the facts before as I considered them very personal and, on reflection, also personal to you although you did not know it.

Unless one lived through the period, it is something no one could really understand. We just seemed to be there every day and somehow drew strength from each other and the gallant ground crew, intelligence officers etc., etc.

I hope when you wrote your book you recorded two facts always wrongly recorded in other books:

(a)   Early in January 1942, AVM Hugh Pughe Lloyd supported by the AOC-in-C MEAF called on Air Ministry to provide a small number of experienced UK fighter pilots to be trained on PR Spitfires to re-establish his PR capability in Malta. Les and I formed part of this reinforcement and we were both trained by No 1 PRU Training Flight at Detling under Sqn

Ldr Watts. I also have always assumed you were part of this small specially selected group. As an established pre-war Civil Servant I made sure I had a copy of this signal when I left the UK – (very prudent of me – but that is a different story). Incidentally, Lloyd, when he took over Bomber Command in the 1950s did precisely the same thing. He brought in fighter personnel to instill some 'rapid reaction' and 'go' into the system. This latter decision was recorded in his official obituary.

(b) On long PR sorties we used to drain the wing tanks to exhaustion i.e. until the engine stopped. One then isolated the appropriate tank and started up the windmilling engine via the main tank and then selected the other wing tank. As you must well recall this business of twice having an engine stop in flight had to be carefully thought out to avoid it happening over the various targets or when highly vulnerable. When both wing tanks were dry and we were over Greece or Benghazi or in between on a shipping search, it was time to come home. There was just enough fuel to stand off for 20 minutes or so if an air raid was in progress on return to Malta.

In conclusion and as an aside while at Luqa one day, AVM Park asked me 'What is all this about the Wing Commander losing his engine and starting it up after losing thousands of feet and then continuing to the target?' I said that the Wng Cdr must have let the fuel cocks ice up and they un-froze at the lower altitude. I then explained the PR fuel system management. As a Spitfire pilot, he was interested, very surprised and said, 'Must give you a heart attack when the engine cuts out.' I smiled and said it was just a case of planning carefully to not let it happen at the wrong time and place and to regularly exercise the fuel cocks to avoid them icing up. He chuckled and said cheerily, 'Very interesting and the best of luck' as he left.

Sorry about the writing but I am due an eye operation next Friday which I hope will restore a measure of improvement to my eyesight.
Very best wishes to you and yours
  Sincerely
  Jo D.

MOVEMENT ORDER
ISSUED TO AUTHOR

R.T. Office,
Central Station,
Bournemouth,
Hampshire,

Date.... 15 Sept 1941

To :-....P/O Coldbeck...........

i/c Draft to......GRANGEMOUTH....

   I have to inform you that you are detailed as..Officer......
         GRANGEMOUTH
i/c Draft proceeding to.................................. and will be
re:_onsible for the conducting of your Draft to that Unit.

   On the train journey from Bour: :outh to.....GRANGEMOUTH........
you will be entirely responsible that no Officer or airman of your
Draft leaves the train and also that you arrive complete with your
Draft at the destination.

   Further, it is pointed out for your information that all
ranks below Officer will be responsible for the handling of their personal
kit at all transitional terminal stations.

   Failure to comply with these orders will be your personal
responsibility and will involve disciplinary action being taken by the
Air Ministry against you from a point of view of neglect of duty.

HSBall
Flight Lieutenant,
R.T.O. Bournemouth.

It is His Majesty's pleasure that you do cause the Air Forces under your command, in so far as authorised by the King's Regulations and Air Council instructions, to proceed, from time to time as occasion shall require, by such routes as you may judge expedient, to or from such place or places as shall be necessary in the performance of their duties.

Wherein the Civil Magistrates, and all others concerned, are to be assisting in providing Quarters, impressing Carriages, and otherwise, as there shall be occasion, according to Law.

Given at the Air Ministry, this 3rd day of July, 1940.

By His Majesty's Command,

(SIGNED) ARCHIBALD SINCLAIR.

To Officers Commanding whom it may concern.

Serial No. ...PRef. K30.

By virtue of the foregoing authority, the following move is authorised for the service specified:-

...P/O A.P. Coldbeck... with ...Seven... officers, ...warrant officers, ...Nineteen... N.C.O.s, and Sgts. ...airmen, ...women, ...children, is ordered to proceed from Bournemouth to Grangemouth ...day on which proceeding... Posting to N° 58 OTU

No. and date of superior authority, if any... Air Ministry D.P.I.

Date.	Departure time	Depart from	Arrive at	Arrival time	Mode of Conveyance	No. of Rly. Wt.
9.41	15.05	Bournemouth	W Waterloo	18.10	Rail	117344
		Waterloo	Kings X		Tube	
	21.45	Kings X	Grangemouth	0859	Rail	

UNIT STAMP

Additional Instructions (if any):- As per attached Roll

Given at Bournemouth, this 15th day of September 1941

Signature... Clim?ton... Rank F/L Adjutant

Where other than the cheapest and most direct route is authorised, railway warrants must be endorsed in red ink to show the alternative route and initialled by the issuing officer.

No. 58 OTU - GRANGEMOUTH -   15.9.41.
Rail Station - GRANGEMOUTH - Colour -
BROWN - Assemble 1600 hours under Squadron

+ NZ P/O H.G. COLDBECK,   : Pilot.
          C.G. EVRISS,   +
          R.H. GRAY,
          V.N. MEARES,
          R.K. MATHISON,
          E.D. MACKIE,   +
          G.   STENBORG, +
      AUS J.R. SLY.   +
        Sgt 400833 REID,   H.R.
            402938 JONES,   G.R.
            403046 FORD,   R.G.
            401872 BUETTEL,   K.N.   BLEAVE
        NZ 404619 McGARRY,   B.R.
            41492 PIERCE,   F.A.
            404349 PENNY,   T.R.
            41630 SULLIVAN,   A.C.
            404988 HOLMES,   N.C.
      CAN   70970 ALDCORN,   W.F.
            73447 BAYCROFT,   T.G.
            80806 BENTLEY,   W.J.
            85860 BALLANTYNE, J.H.
            80134 EBY,   W.H.
            77332 WARENNE,   P.E.
            77220 MOUNT,   L.
            69243 NAPUER,   G.C.
            80074 NOVAK,   W.L.
            70211 SEIVERT,   H.O.

INDEX